THE CRITICAL
MISSED
STEP

GERALDINE E. RODGERS

authorHOUSE®

AuthorHouse™
1663 Liberty Drive
Bloomington, IN 47403
www.authorhouse.com
Phone: 833-262-8899

Published by AuthorHouse   08/05/2022

ISBN: 978-1-5462-2806-6 (sc)
ISBN: 978-1-5462-2805-9 (e)

Print information available on the last page.

"Syllabis nullum compendium est, perdiscendae omnis."
Quintilian, 35-100 A.D.

CONTENTS

INTRODUCTION

Back in the early 19ᵗʰ century, a culture-destroying, upside-down change was being massively promoted in the English-speaking world on both sides of the Atlantic. It is astonishing, not only that the change was successfully promoted, but that it left so few historical tracks.

We are still reeling from its cultural and other effects, such as damaged conditioned reflexes. Yet almost no one knows that a cultural change occurred and that it was catastrophic. That is because, with Mephistophelian lying skill, the "experts" who promoted it also sold it as a huge improvement. To this very day, the few who do know about that "improvement", innocently think it was good. Also, this writer formerly thought that some of its damage had been reasonably minimized but now realizes that its damage is impossible to remove. So this awful "improvement" remains today. It is as culturally unchallenged as the hideous foot-binding of little girls' feet was unchallenged in China for so many centuries, but today it is brains that are being permanently bound.

What was this watershed and enormously harmful change which has been misunderstood or ignored for so very long, for some 200 years? Before answering that question, something should be considered that has been very truly said. It is that, in order for an answer to a question to be understood correctly, an inquirer must already know about 90% of the answer that is to be given. Therefore, it will be worthwhile first to review some of that necessary 90% background of knowledge.

WHAT IS FUNCTIONAL ILLITERACY?

Concerning part of the background, few people know that we have a so-called "functional" illiteracy problem. Of the relatively few who do know, almost no one knows the massive extent of that problem, or the nature of the problem, itself.

It would be reasonable to conclude that "functional" illiteracy must mean that there are literate people who can read fluently but who are, because of some defect, incapable of understanding what they are reading. Such a condition does, of course, exist but more commonly with computer software than with human beings. Computer software can read aloud anything that is printed here with quick and astonishing accuracy but is incapable of understanding any of it. However, a vast group of true "functional" illiterates are very different from the two groups just mentioned, the people with defective understanding, and the computers with no understanding. With this third group, the problem is not that they cannot understand what is written, which is true of the first two groups. With the third group of "functional" illiterates, the problem is that they cannot read all of what is written, and that is why they cannot understand.

Almost no one knows that about 75% of anything spoken or written in English is composed of words from a very short list of the 300 most frequently used words. Almost no one knows that more than 90% of anything that is spoken or written in English is composed of words from a short list of the 1,000 most frequently used words. English, of course, has a vastly greater vocabulary than a mere 1,000 words, and instead has a probable total of far over a half million words.

Healthy listeners can hear 100% of anything made up of words from that over-half-million list of English words. They can hear very well even the English words that are the rarest and the most difficult, probably words that they had never heard before. However, those same healthy listeners might not do so well if those same words are given to them in writing. They may not be able to "hear" some of those words when they are written, even though they had no trouble at all hearing those words when they were spoken. Some listeners, when they try to read, are unable to "hear" a vast number of written words which they have no trouble hearing when they are spoken. For instance, a very intelligent middle-aged woman I knew, a college graduate, told me that she skipped over all the "hard" words when she was reading!

"Reading experts" say that a reader who knows only 90% of the sight words on a page may be able to read that page "above the frustration level" for understanding. Therefore, since words from the list of the thousand most frequently used words compose a little more than 90% of almost anything, a reader who knows only those thousand words may be able to read many things "above the frustration level" for understanding. Such a reader context-guesses correctly at least the meaning of the words he cannot read, the remaining 10%, from the 90% he can read from the list of the thousand most common words. With the help of jig-saw-puzzle "phonics," which is the piecing together of parts from already "learned" words, or using beginning letter sounds to context-guess, he also may be able to figure out what many of those unknown 10% of the words actually are, as in, "Mary had a little l…..".

Even though that reader could not read 10% of the printed words in the selection if they were out of that context and on a printed list, he can be passed along as being literate. The reason is that he could very probably answer "reading comprehension questions" correctly if the selection is simple enough. Such tests of so-called "reading comprehension" are the standard test for reading ability today. Yet, of course, he certainly is not literate since the English language has over half a million words. While words taken from the list of the 1,000 most frequent do form 90% of almost anything, a truly successful reader is able to "hear" and so to pronounce aloud, not just those words, but all of the words in the selection, even if he does not know their meanings. A truly successful reader can read aloud just as accurately as computer software can read, and for the same reason, because he has been correctly "programmed" to read the sounds of syllables in words, and the very occasional truly irregular words (such as "one").

It is when material becomes harder to understand, even if a reader does know those thousand most frequently used words (and perhaps many more), that such context-guessing on the meaning of the more difficult unknown words may no longer work. Of course, the more intelligent a word-guesser is, and the more words above 1,000 frequency that he knows, the longer the context-guessing process will continue to work, but at some point it breaks down for almost all of them.

It is only when a reader fails those "reading comprehension" questions on more difficult content (which means when guessing fails to work), that he joins the ranks of what are euphemistically called the "functional" illiterates. Yet no one ever tests his oral reading accuracy to see if the problem is that he cannot really read all of the words. All that he is given is silent reading followed by the pernicious "silent reading comprehension" questions. Those "silent reading comprehension" questions really only test intelligence, not reading ability, but they have served to mask our true illiteracy problem ever since 1914.

The psychologist, Alfred Binet of France, composed about 1908 what may have been the first intelligence texts. A portion of his tests used oral reading, followed by oral questioning on the content that was orally read, as one measure of intelligence. Until Binet first introduced those "reading comprehension questions," so far as can be determined, "reading comprehension tests" had never existed. However, Binet and his assistant, Simon, were amazed by the fact that some exceedingly disabled readers were still able to answer correctly Binet's "reading comprehension questions", even though their oral reading could not be understood by Binet and Simon because they missed so many words. The fact that Binet's disabled readers missed so many words suggests that they may even have been reading below that 90% word accuracy - the so-called "frustration level" of the reading experts. Yet, since they answered the "reading comprehension questions" correctly, they might today be considered to be "successful" readers, not "functional illiterates"! (Pedagogie Experimentale by Dr. Theophile Simon, Librairie Armand Colin, Paris, France, 1924)

So Binet, who seems to have been the inventor of "reading comprehension questions", only used that invention as a way to test intelligence, not reading ability. Obviously, being able to pass "reading comprehension questions" is no guarantee at all that a subject can actually read. We have Binet and Simon's implicit admission that "reading comprehension tests" are meaningful only to evaluate intelligence, not literacy. The only test of literacy is the ability to pronounce words in print.

THE BUSY-BODY ACTIVISTS OF 1914-1930 ENTER THE SCENE, WITH A LONG AND DISMAL BACKGROUND BEHIND THEM

A normal question to ask at this point is, "Why then are children - and whole classes - not given oral reading tests, to find if the children - and the classes - can or cannot pronounce words in print?" Why not, indeed? Why are oral reading accuracy tests with easily understandable, standardized grade-level averages missing in American education? Why have such class tests been unknown for over a hundred years, when, at that very same time, schools have been inundated, almost drowned, by the so-called "silent reading comprehension" tests?

"Silent reading comprehension tests" were invented over a century ago by America's earliest psychologists. One of those early psychologists in 1914 was Edward L. Thorndike of Columbia Teachers College in New York City. Thorndike's 1914 graduate student, William Scott Gray, later went to the University of Chicago, and, while there in 1930, published the first deaf-mute method readers, the Scott, Foresman famous "Dick and Jane" series. That reading series later blanketed the entire United States for about 25 years. It quickly wiped out the many reading series that had preceded it, which had been listed in The United States Catalog - Books in Print January 1, 1928 (Fourth Edition, The H. W. Wilson Company, New York, 1928). That post-1930 massive take-over of American reading instruction, and the removal of those multiple earlier series, stands as an unspoken testimony to the enormous influence of the circa 1914-1930 education "experts."

It is interesting that perhaps the oldest and perhaps the most widely used oral reading accuracy tests were written in 1913-1914 by Gray, himself, for his master's degree taken directly under Thorndike at Columbia Teachers College in New York. The tests were partially revised by 1916 and were included in what was apparently Gray's 1916 doctoral thesis at the University of Chicago, published by the university in 1917 as "Studies of Elementary Reading," part of Supplementary Educational Monographs, No. 1-6. (See Appendix A for Gray's 1916 test paragraphs and circa-1916 testing scores.)

Gray had constructed the 1913-1914 original oral reading accuracy tests directly under Professor Thorndike, who was then writing some of the earliest reading comprehension tests. (The extensive bibliography to Gray's 1916 thesis lists similar "comprehension" work at that time by others than Thorndike. Gray's 1916 bibliography is a window to the "expert" world of that time.) In 1915 and possibly 1916, Gray's tests, with some revisions, were used for testing in city school surveys in Cleveland and Grand Rapids, and most probably in other places. There were further revisions before 1916. The circa-1916 tests and test results were reported in Gray's "Studies of Elementary Reading", published in 1917 as shown above. His circa-1916 statistics clearly showed that 100% of the sixth-graders tested about 1916 could read at least simple materials. There was no illiteracy in those sixth grades. However, Gray did not publish such clear statistics for his tests at the third, fourth, and fifth grades. Instead, he gave queer sorts of averages for all grades lumped together, but even those suggest high scoring at all grades.

If the individual scores Gray had received at all grades had been reported by Gray, as he did report for at least the sixth-grade scores, that material could have had great use. Gray's test results from the actual testing of circa-1916 3rd. 4th, 5th and 6th grades could have made it possible to see how accurately an average child could read in 1916, at what was a confirmed 3rd, 4th, 5th or 6th grade level of accuracy in 1916. It would then be possible to give the same tests to today's children, and to see how they compared to those tested in 1916. The results should be appalling.

Gray's test results could have provided that useful, reality-based grade-level scale by which to evaluate present–day individual scores. However, so far as I know, Gray never published concrete data for all grade levels tested about 1916, but did so only for the sixth grade.

Gray's reading test was published for very many years after 1916 in different editions, with a final revision written by Gray before he died. Even up to today, his test is still being revised and republished. However, for a very long time, "reading comprehension questions" and even other factors have been added to the test and have been weighed into the complicated scoring. This "improvement" of adding "reading comprehension ability" to what is supposed to be an oral reading accuracy score is obviously ridiculous. However, so far as I know, none of the editions of the Gray test published after 1917 gave anything like the clear scoring method for simple reading accuracy that Gray used for sixth grades in 1916.

What "functional" illiteracy usually means in practice is that many people with 100% of normal hearing are able to "hear" only 90% or so of language if it is written. They are effectively partial deaf-mutes when faced with print. There is a dismal but largely unknown historical background behind the very ugly fact that our government schools (actually since about 1826, not just 1930) have turned so many students into partial deaf-mutes (with a respite from about 1895 or so to 1930). As will be shown, the historical damage to American literacy did not result just from the Thorndike/Gray/Gates deaf-mute-method readers of 1930-1931, but from a large group of activists far earlier, in the early 19th century. However, from about 1895 to 1930, the introduction in American schools of what was called "supplemental phonics", and true phonics in spelling books after about 1885 or so, had overcome most of the damage. Yet the 1930-1931 texts, using instead what they labeled "intrinsic phonics," (a form of context-guessing) and new and appalling non-phonic spelling books, removed all that successful material.

A great deal of self-justifying talk comes from "experts" that our government schools today do teach so-called phonics (sound) to "decode" unknown words, but what they are promoting does not really make it possible for children to "hear" print. Basal reader phonics is normally only the conscious pulling apart and re-assembling the parts of already memorized sight-words, jig-saw puzzle phonics, using the context of the selection to confirm guesses on the new word's identity.

While the 1930-1931 deaf-mute readers are clearly modeled on Thomas Gallaudet's <u>The Mother's Primer</u> of 1835, the Gallaudet reader did not use the jig-saw-puzzle phonics approach, but only context-guessing. Jig-saw-puzzle phonics did go back to 18th century France, but Gallaudet did not use it. It only blossomed anew about the time of the 1875 "improvements" in Boston and Quincy (another sad story, too long for here.)

Gallaudet wrote <u>The Mother's Primer</u> with the same whole-sight-word, context-guessing method that he had used in his famous school for deaf-mutes, but he was promoting the book's use, not just for deaf children, but for hearing children as well. What Gallaudet did use in that book almost constantly was the 90% "guessing" frustration level. Children could presumably guess the meaning of a "new" word if it were in a sufficiently long context of already known words, a context of 90% or so of known words. That circa 90% presumption is based on the fact that a word count of <u>The Mother's Primer</u> shows that Gallaudet almost always introduced new words only when those new words amounted to 10% or less of their context.

A word count would probably also show that, like Gray/Gates and the deaf-mute method readers, Gallaudet's "new" words were then repeated a sufficient number of times so that they could be embedded in the reader's memory. The word-counting of repetitions was one of the most appalling clerical jobs in the 1930-1931 deaf-mute method Gray and Gates readers. Their "stories" had to give a sufficient number of repetitions for each new word. An unfortunate group of people must have spent a great deal of time counting the words in the Dick and Jane "literature," and, if a new word had not been repeated enough, trying to fit in its missing "repeats" somewhere in the already awful "literature."

Back in the 18th century, Charles Lamb, the famous author, had something to say about such impoverished, unnatural "literature" for children, when normal syntax and vocabulary was deliberately omitted, presumably to make it more suitable for young minds. Victor E. Neuburg in his book, The Penny Histories, Harcourt, Brace & World, Inc., 1968, (page 53-55), referred to some children's books that were popular in England about 1800, which Neuburg said were:

> "...written by the imitators of Hannah More and 'the cursed Barbauld Crew, those Blights and Blasts of all that is Human in man and child,' as Lamb characterized them."

Certainly Lamb would put Gray, Gates and their followers in that same literature-mangling "Barbauld Crew."

Gallaudet's 1835 primer was published shortly after a huge drive in the English-speaking world denigrating the use of the age-old "sound" syllable tables for beginning children and instead promoting the teaching of sight words for "meaning". Gallaudet's primer not only omitted the syllable tables but omitted any thing at all to do with the sounds of words.

An open, publicized drive in English against dependence on syllable sounds and promoting dependence on word meanings (for hearing children) is best dated to beginning in 1826. However, the drive did begin to surface visibly in English about 1818, and its English-language roots go back even further to Richard Lovell Edgeworth in Ireland (1744-1817) in his Essays on Practical Education, 1798, and his 1799 A Rational Primer. Edgeworth strongly opposed the use of the syllabary for beginning readers.

In the German language, Johann Bernhard Basedow, in his famous Philanthropinum School founded in 1774 in Dessau, Germany, was the first well-known proponent of whole words instead of the syllable tables for beginning readers. However, Basedow did also successfully use "sound" with Pascal letter-naming phonics. Basedow inspired a host of other programs in the German language, out of which grew the widely used and successful analytic-synthetic phonic word method, a "sound"-based approach.

In the French language, whole-word roots for beginners go back even further to what may have been the very first such author, M. de Vallange, New Systems or New Plans of Methods to Succeed Quickly and Easily.... in France in 1719.

Out of Villange's 1719 work apparently grew Abbe Bertaud's Quadrille des Enfants whole-word method in France in 1744. Bertaud's 1744 work apparently inspired a great many other whole-word methods in the French language, through the 18th and early 19th centuries, including the famous Abbe de l'Epee's method in his school in Paris, France, for deaf mutes, where Gallaudet trained. However, other than in de l'Epee's materials for deaf-mutes, apparently few of the French programs were ever widely used. (Source: Dictionnaire de Pedagogie et d'Instruction Primaire [1880-1888], Paris, France.)

While Basedow's method used Pascal phonics, and was therefore successful, Bertaud and some of the French versions largely used the jig-saw-puzzle approach, pulling apart and putting together pieces of already memorized whole words to work out unknown words. That, of course, is a silent method that can be used to teach deaf-mutes.

The jig-saw-puzzle "phonics" method was pushed into the Boston schools by the September, 1878, Boston curriculum guide, anonymous portions of which do sound like William James's prose. Leigh (true) phonics was thrown out. It had been only a few months before, on March 1, 1878 that the award-winning Boston Schools Superintendent John Dudley Philbrick (1818-1886), had been fired by his enemies. It had been Philbrick who had introduced phonic methods, and eventually the highly successful Leigh phonics, in place of the sight-word method. (See my book, The Hidden Story.) Philbrick and his Leigh phonics departed from the Boston schools almost simultaneously.

In his earlier 1874 Boston Annual Schools Report, pages 283-285, Philbrick had referred to the 1826 switch from the use of the syllable tables which had taken placed some thirty years before he became superintendent in 1857. Philbrick wrote:

"In respect to the initiating of children into the art and mystery of reading, - the teaching of them the elements of the art, the enabling of them to pronounce at sight the words of easy prose or verse, - I found the Primary Schools on my first inspection of them in 1857, in a deplorable condition. The old-fashioned method, by ABC syllables and spelling, had been nominally abolished by the abolition of the usual appliances for teaching it, and it had been so much ridiculed that the teachers were very shy in using it in the presence of visitors. The reading books and charts in the schools were designed for the 'word-method,' a method of very limited capabilities… In recalling the slow and tedious processes by which they brought their pupils up into only semi-fluent reading, I am reminded of what Milton says of an arduous path,

> "'Long is the way,
>   And hard, that out of Hell leads up to light.'"

"All that has been changed, but long and hard has been the road by which the change has been reached….. the teachers were gradually initiated into the phonic method…"

It was almost immediately after Philbrick had been fired that the highly successful Leigh phonics was replaced by the jig-saw-puzzle phonics outlined in the new, September, 1878, Boston curriculum guide. A puzzled comment was made at that time by school personnel (cited in my Hidden Story) that all the Leigh print reading books had disappeared from the Boston schools over the summer of 1878, along with the records of children's achievement.

Jig-saw-puzzle phonics appeared in the 1920's, in the supposedly new "intrinsic" phonics of Arthur I. Gates of Columbia Teachers College. "Intrinsic phonics" was nothing but context-guessing, assisted by jig-saw-puzzle phonics. Gates' "intrinsic phonics method" was used by him in his 1931 deaf-mute-method Macmillan readers and by Gray in his 1930 deaf-mute-method Scott, Foresman readers.

It should be self-evident that the "experts" never called the 1930/1931 readers what they clearly intended them to be: deaf-mute-method readers. Yet there can be no doubt, as shown by Gates' own writings in his 1930 book, Interest and Ability in Reading, about elaborate work that was done to adapt deaf-mute beginning reading materials for use as beginning reading materials for hearing children. The implication is that it was those adapted materials that were used in writing Gates' Macmillan series that was published in 1931.

The jig-saw-puzzle method lives on today, unchallenged, as the fake so-called "phonics" in today's American schools. A government-funded test of adults' reading skills to be discussed later showed that jig-saw-puzzle phonics is what most adult American readers today use when reading.

So Gray's 1930 and Gates' 1931 readers were only an extension - and elaboration - of the 1826 drive in English, and an extension of similar whole-word methods that had been promoted in eighteenth-century France. Yet there was something startlingly new about the method used in Gray's 1930 and Gates' 1931 texts. They were using something that was new on the face of the earth for hearing children.

Gray's and Gates' former professor, Thorndike, had spent ten long years (1911-1921) compiling a list of the 10,000 commonest words in their order of frequency, something never done before, although Leonard Ayres, in his A Measuring Scale for Ability in Spelling, Russell Sage Foundation, New York, had published the 1,000 word level by 1915. Thorndike's list of the 10,000 commonest words had finally made it possible to write a reading series to the sixth grade without using any true sound at all, but only meaning-bearing sight words and jig-saw-puzzle, silent "phonics." Before Thorndike's list became available, some true phonics or sound always had to be introduced for hearing children in teaching reading, after the first- grade level.

What sort of crippled thinking could make it preferable to omit all sound in the teaching of reading? The 1913 Volume 3 of A Cyclopedia of Education, New York, contains an article, "Teaching Beginners to Read," by Henry Suzzallo, then of Columbia Teachers College where Thorndike worked, and the article explains the reasoning quite clearly.

The article shows a conditioned-reflex type of triangle, with three possible sequential steps in a learned response. The steps could be taken either in a clockwise or a counter–clockwise direction. The triangle is labeled at the top point, Meaning, and at the bottom two points, Visual on the right side and Sound on the left side. (See the illustration on the next page.)

The first clockwise step on the bottom line on the triangle, between Visual (print) and Sound (oral reading), is very short, suggesting that the first clockwise step is easy. Since the lines from the bottom to the top point are far longer, that suggests that the second clockwise step, from Sound to Meaning, which is the ultimate goal, is more difficult.

The psychologist's assumption at this point is almost self-evident: If the steps on the triangle are taken in a clockwise direction, children might read flawlessly (from Visual print to Sound oral reading) but never take that effort-filled long step up to Meaning. They did not need to think about what it was that they were pronouncing so flawlessly.

However, if the triangle steps are taken in a counter-clockwise direction, starting at Visual (print), the first counter-clockwise step has to go from Visual (print) directly up to Meaning on the long and therefore more difficult line. However, Sound (accuracy in oral reading) would then become an unnecessary after-thought once Meaning, the ultimate goal, has been achieved. The assumption must have been that it was not necessary for children to take the effort-filled step on the long, final, downward counter-clockwise move, from Meaning to Sound.

Obviously, if someone approved of the counter-clockwise route, then accuracy in oral reading, as could be shown by Gray's original oral reading tests, was of virtually no importance. Therefore, note the post-1914 virtual elimination of oral reading accuracy testing in American schools!

The importance of Meaning, of course (so-called "reading comprehension") was Thorndike's hobby-horse, as it was for his ex-professor, the psychologist, William James of Harvard. This writer believes that the Reading Triangle was devised long before 1913, by William James himself, an avowed materialist like his student, Thorndike.

THE READING TRIANGLE

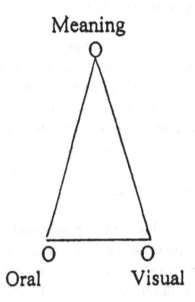

Meaning

Oral   Visual

Source: Article entitled, "Reading, Teaching Beginners"
by Henry Suzzallo, on page 118 of the 1913 volume of
A Cyclopedia of Education, edited by Paul Monroe,
Columbia University. Suzzallo was also with Columbia,
at Teachers College, and had been a graduate student of
the psychologist, E. L. Thorndike ,at Columbia about 1901.
Thorndike had been a graduate student of the psychologist,
James McKeen Cattell, at Columbia in 1898, and of
the psychologist, William James, at Harvard,
before that.

William James wrote a paper, in 1904, <u>Does Consciousness Exist?</u> In it, he said:

> "The word consciousness is just a loose way of indicating that certain sensory occurrences form part of my life history."

By the time James wrote this 1904 paper, he had obviously become a complete materialist.

When Thorndike was a graduate student at Harvard in the 1890's, he kept his "experimental chickens" in the basement of William James' home. Therefore, Thorndike's relationship with James must have been quite close, which probably explains why Thorndike's work sometimes sounds like warmed-over James. For a 1908 book, <u>Essays Philosophical and Psychological in Honor of William James</u>, Thorndike wrote a chapter, "A Pragmatic Substitute for Free Will." In it, he reportedly discussed free will by such things as instinctive responses and the resultant habits developing from them. It appears that Thorndike threw consciousness into the discard, just as James did.

If it is assumed to have been unfortunate that confused men such as James and Thorndike had great influence on public (government) schools, that assumption is very badly turned around. What was unfortunate was the existence of the organized network of government schools which made it possible for confused men such as James and Thorndike to wield such great influence. They could do so with virtually no informed parental opposition.

Since James and Thorndike were complete materialists, they had no room in their logic for anything like voluntary attention or voluntary inattention on Meaning when reading printed words, because they denied the existence of free will (which permits voluntary action). They saw the human mind as just an involuntary machine, and explained it with just so many gears, as in the Reading Triangle.

The record indicates that these psychological busy-bodies from the early twentieth century thought that "reading comprehension" was damaged by the phonic method (Visual to Sound to Meaning), as readers might pronounce the words correctly at Sound, but fail too often to finish the cycle by going to Meaning. The use of free consciousness to make that second step from Sound to Meaning was an impossibility to them since they denied the very existence of consciousness and its free will. Every action had to be automatically and unthinkingly produced by a skill, or by a complicated mesh of previous skills.

Therefore, to protect the achievement of Meaning (so-called reading comprehension) from being stalled at the Sound stop, they promoted the deaf-mute method, because it is a one-step method, which goes silently from Visual, the printed word, directly to the print's Meaning. Of course, it is true that the meaning of an isolated printed word, if learned without sound, can be automatically produced from the brain's memory banks, just as looking at a picture of an apple produces the meaning of that object from the brain's automatic memory banks. But such resurrected memories are only the building blocks of language, or syntax. Such isolated items can rarely produce syntax, or language, and it is only completed syntax which presents meaning to consciousness for understanding. It is not the length of the syntax, which matters, but only the presence of it. For instance, "Apple," has no syntax, but the following, with fewer letters, does: Help!

Therefore, while the deaf mute method of reading isolated printed words without any sound attached to them is probably automatic, understanding the meaning of sentences (syntax) containing those words cannot be automatic. Reading skill, properly achieved, is a conditioned reflex and Meaning should occur (or not occur) only after the skill has been exercised. Like all conditioned reflexes, reading can be done with or without the use of conscious attention, just as is true with walking. However, to focus too much conscious attention on the act of walking can produce stumbling. Focusing too much (or any) conscious attention on the act or reading can also produce a kind of stumbling. That divided attention produces a reduction in the ability to take all of the meaning from what is being read.

The Meaning method they promoted is demonstrably inferior in producing accurate reading, but it is defended by the claim that it produces improved, so-called "reading comprehension". Yet the term, "reading comprehension", is an oxymoron, a contradiction in terms, which means it is something that does not really exist. Reading skill - turning print into language - is a conditioned (learned) skill (or should be), carried out in what the neurologist Dr. Wilder Penfield called the brain's automatic sensory-motor mechanism. That brain area which stores skills, has no consciousness at all, any more than a computer has, so it cannot "comprehend" anything. (The Mystery of the Mind, Princeton University, Princeton, New Jersey, 1975) Comprehension is carried out in the brain's Higher Brain Mechanism, where consciousness resides and which does not contain conditioned skills, so it cannot, by definition, contain any such "skill" as so-called "reading comprehension." However, these experts" denied the very existence of consciousness in the brain! In effect, they saw the entire brain as an "automatic sensory-motor mechanism"!

These materialists, who denied the existence of free will and even of consciousness in the mind (!!!!), became very busy after about 1911 protecting their so-called and utterly senseless "reading comprehension skill" by denigrating and working against phonic, Sound, approaches, and promoting the Visual to Meaning approaches - the sight-word method.

By the end of the first three grades with Gray's materials, an astonishingly small vocabulary had been taught - only about 2,000 words, presumably the most commonly used words in English. Of course, that would mean the critical 1,000 commonest had been taught, so the children could then be reading "above the frustration level" for guessing unknown words The massively used (and detestable) "reading workbooks" in the government schools would continue for years, to give children massive practice in guessing unknown words in written contexts. They would then be able to pass the fake "reading comprehension tests" at what is so wrongly labeled, "grade level," instead of intelligence level.

So William Scott Gray's deaf-mute-method readers with controlled high-frequency vocabulary to the sixth grade only became possible to write because Edward L. Thorndike had spent ten long years (1911-1921) counting the frequency of words in print. Since it was such a ghastly job for ten long years, Thorndike certainly must have been highly motivated to do it because of some goal. That goal must have been to make it possible to teach hearing children as if they were deaf-mutes, without the use of any "sound" at all and totally dependent on "meaning." (As has been mentioned, Thorndike's ex-professor, William James of Harvard, is the apparent source for Thorndike's deaf-mute-method "meaning" ideas. James' 1890 text, The Principles of Psychology, makes it clear that he was fascinated with the soundless thinking of deaf-mutes. See my Hidden Story.)

It was in 1921 that Thorndike finally produced a list of the 10,000 highest-frequency words in their order of frequency. However, after Thorndike had started his count in 1911, by 1915, the 1,000 commonest words were listed in their order of frequency by Leonard P. Ayres in his A Measuring Scale for Ability in Spelling, Russell Sage Foundation, New York. It is meaningful that the Ayres' spelling scale showed vastly, vastly higher spelling accuracy in 1915 than after the 1930-1931 deaf-mute method type of readers had taken over in America. After about 1940, many other deaf-mute-method series besides the first ones were published. The resulting drop in spelling ability as a result of all the deaf-mute-method readers is almost unbelievable, as shown by comparing the spelling accuracy scores in 1954 on The New Iowa Spelling Scale to the spelling accuracy scores for the same words if they were on Ayres' 1915 tests. (See Appendix B.)

Arthur Irving Gates wrote an article, before the 1930 deaf-mute-method texts were published, explaining their "intrinsic phonics", which was jig-saw-puzzle phonics, using parts of already learned sight words plus context guessing. ("The Supplementary Device Versus the Intrinsic Method of Teaching Reading," Elementary School Journal, University of Chicago, June, 1925.) Guessing "intrinsic phonics" replaced the true phonic "supplementary" drill that had been used from circa 1895 to 1930 in America. No longer did first- and second-grade children get the daily phonic drill that had been the norm from charts in the room, very often on window shades that were rolled down and up.

Thorndike's high-frequency word list had finally made it possible for William Scott Gray and Thorndike's other Columbia Teacher's College ex-student, Arthur Irving Gates, to write the first deaf-mute-method series to sixth grade, the 1930 Scott, Foresman (Gray's) and the 1931 Macmillan (Gates') reading series. Those texts had totally controlled vocabulary so that all children could now be taught to read like deaf-mutes, by word meanings in guessing contexts, not by word sounds.

THE OMISSION OF THE SYLLABLE STEP

As discussed, Thorndike, Gray, et al, in 1914-1930, were only building on the work of an earlier group, Gallaudet et al, from circa 1826, who also had promoted "meaning" as all important in beginning reading. Yet what Gallaudet omitted - and what Gray et al also omitted - was the very beginning step in learning spoken language, the syllable step. That had been the beginning step in learning to read since about 800 B. C., and apparently until the arrival of whole-word "meaning" in France with M. de Vallange in 1719.

Syllables have no meaning, as words do. A baby begins to say ma ma, wa wa, etc., and it is only AFTER he has learned those syllable sounds that he attaches meaning to them. So syllables, not words, are the very first step in learning to speak and the evidence to be given demonstrates that syllables should also be the very first step in learning to read.

For thousands of years, syllables had been the very first step in learning to read, once the vowel-containing alphabet had been learned. It is intriguing that, in those thousands of years, almost no comments have survived that indicate any trouble in learning to read, any more than in learning to speak.

It should be pointed out that there is no such thing as an isolated consonant letter sound, except for a few like m. The word itself, consonant, means "with" something, and that something is a vowel letter (a, e, i, o, u), to produce a syllable. Syllables formed with consonants plus vowels, and syllables formed with the vowels alone, are the fundamental, unbreakable units in language. For thousands of years, children were taught to construct those syllables from a written alphabet table, such as pointing to "b" and naming it, and then to "a" and naming it, and then saying the syllable they form, "ba." The chant from fairy tales in English, "Fe, fi, fo, fum, I smell the blood of an Englishman," is evidence that it was normal for English-speaking children centuries ago to be very familiar with the syllable table. What is particularly striking is that the chant is with the "f" syllables, the very spot at which the "given" printed syllable tables on the children's horn book ended, after which the children would find it more difficult to construct the remaining alphabetic syllables by themselves from the alphabet table at the top of the horn book.

Obviously, the syllable is fundamental in speech. What, then, is the full sequence of steps in producing speech and listening to speech? Since reading should be only a form of listening to speech, and writing should be only a form of producing speech, then the full sequence of steps for the reading and writing of sound-bearing alphabetic print should be the same as for listening to speech and for producing speech. Therefore, what is that necessary background with which to explain those steps that should be the same for both speech and writing?

For thousands of years, the steps for both spoken speech and written speech remained identical and unchanged. That is, they remained identical and unchanged until the so-called Age of Enlightenment which brought with it such "improvements" as the French Revolution. One of those "improvements" from the so-called "Enlightenment" of men such as Voltaire was a presumed"new" way to teach beginning reading - by the meaning of alphabetically-written whole words instead of by the sound of alphabetically-written isolated syllables. While that French method originated as early as 1719, it did not really become important until after 1744.

Of course, by ignoring the syllable and depending on "meaning", Progress had taken a massive step backwards. Progress went backward to before circa 800 B. C., before the invention of five vowels in Ancient Greece had finally made it possible to write syllable sounds precisely with the even far-more-ancient Egyptian-invented consonants. Some lengthy syllabaries have been invented in history, but none have the incredible efficiency of our short alphabet (presently 26 letters) of consonants plus vowels, with which it is possible, to construct all the syllables necessary to write down any human thought. Yet, after the renewal of the ancient whole-word method for written language, the first step in learning spoken language, the syllable and the syllable tables, were no longer the first step in learning written language.

Before the invention of the vowels, alphabetic print could be read only by context-guessing of its probable meaning, (guessing of whole words) as there was no way to produce correct syllable sounds. With only consonants to use, context-guessing approximation of whole words was all that was possible, as with "Th cw jmpd vr th mn."

The "meaning" method and its variations were only lightly used in Europe from circa 1744 to the 1790's, but they arrived in the English-speaking world in force by the mid 1820's. However, with the 18th century "new" way to teach reading, by word "meaning," instead of by syllable "sound", the Enlightenment brought something else that was new. It brought functional illiteracy wherever the method was used, because memorizing sight words can be very difficult for many people even when jig-saw-puzzle whole-word "phonics" is used (building "new" words from parts of "old" words). Why did such a seemingly small difference, a lack of emphasis on syllable sounds and a heavy emphasis on word meaning, produce such a huge problem? It is necessary to consider those very real steps that are taken, in listening and speaking, to understand why the sequence of steps are so critically altered.

First, consider listening. A listener's understanding of heard speech begins when his brain's automatic sensory- motor mechanism processes the syllable sounds he is hearing. He does NOT hear "words" first, but deals with syllables first, automatically, and does so in an area in the front left side of the brain, called Broca's area. (It was almost 200 years ago that a man in France named Broca identified some cases of aphasia, or inability to speak, when the aphasics could not imitate speech sounds, as the result of damage to that part of the brain.)

The listener's automatic sensory-motor mechanism then proceeds (if possible) from those heard syllable sounds to construct a syntax which may or may not generate word meanings. Back in the 19th century, a German named Wernicke identified some other cases of aphasia. Those aphasics could handle speech sounds but could not attach word meanings to those speech sounds, as a result of damage to a different area on the left side of the brain, now called Wernicke's area.

The word meanings usually, but not always, appear after syllable sounds have been heard which automatically produce a syntax. When a complete syntax/word product (or isolated word) is generated by a listener's automatic sensory-motor system from those syllable sounds, his conscious brain (his higher-brain mechanism) can then perceive any meaning that syntax/word product (or isolated word) may or may not contain. Of course, the speed of these sequential, automatic steps is very great.

Concerning the automaticity of syntax, it has been recorded that some people who totally lost the ability to understand spoken language, but who retained the ability to mimic it, corrected bad grammar when repeating it as, presumably, such as "You was here" to "You were here." Since they had no conscious understanding of language, their grammar corrections must have been done by an automatic portion of their brains which must deal with syntax. (Source: p. 22, Two Sides of the Brain, Brain Lateralization Explained, Sid J. Seaglowitz, Prentice-Hall, Inc., Englewood Cliffs, New Jersey, 1983)

The sequence of steps for a producer of speech appear to be the same as for a listener to speech, but in reverse. For a producer of speech, it begins with meaning in the producer's conscious brain, which conscious brain then calls on his brain's automatic sensory-motor mechanism to produce first a finished syntax/word product (Wernicke's area) which then proceeds to the syllables to carry the syntax/word product (Broca's area).

Since research has shown the right brain can be used for sight-word "meaning" trained readers, as for Japanese people using the Kanji "meaning" symbols, possibly the right brain may have an area analogous to the Wernicke area on the left side of the brain.

Yet, Lewis Carroll cleverly pointed out something about syntax (Chapter I of Through the Looking Glass, and What Alice Found There). Lewis Carroll showed that excellent syntax may still produce absolutely no meaning, if the syntax generates no meaningful words but only abstract parts of grammar.

> "Twas brillig, and the slithy toves
> Did gyre and gimble in the wabe;
> All mimsy were the borogroves,
> And the mome raths outgrabe."

The syntax is marvelous, but meaning is almost totally missing. However, words alone, without any syntax, produce little meaning. (Rat, down, yesterday).

The terms, automatic sensory-motor mechanism and higher-brain mechanism were used by the neurologist, Dr. Wilder Penfield, in his book The Mystery of the Mind (Princeton University Press, 1975). I have used that source and others to suggest that the above outline may correctly state the sequence of steps in speaking and listening.

Diagrams showing Broca's Area and Wernicke's Area are reproduced in The Principles of Psychology, (Henry Holt and Company, Inc., 1890) by William James, Thorndike's professor and close friend. On page 37, James reproduced Figure 18 showing these areas, taken from an 1887 book, On Aphasia, by James Ross. On page 25, James showed an even clearer illustration of both areas in Figure 11.

The only writing system capable of fully duplicating speech (syllables, to syntax/word product, to meaning, or the reverse steps) is the alphabetic system. (The Japanese writing system uses both Kana syllable characters and Kanji word-meaning-characters. Yet, since they use both, presumably the Kana syllable characters alone could not fully produce all speech.)

Therefore, methods to transfer speech to writing which are wrongly based as a first level on word meaning instead of on the natural first level, syllable sounds, are mangling the natural sequence for the production of speech in the brain by omitting what is the correct first level, the level of sound-bearing syllables (Broca's level). Making "meaning" the first level (Wernicke's level which deals with whole words) leaves unused the sound level. That automatically introduces meaning-based context guessing, and context guessing is prone to error.

When we learn anything, it is stored in the brain. We learn and then store conditioned reflexes for walking, tying our shoelaces, typing, etc. We learn and then store conditioned reflexes for reading, and children who are taught to read whole words for meaning are obviously not starting at the "sound" level, even if the sounds of letters are used in teaching those words. It is still the whole word which is the central focus, not the syllable sounds making that word.

Children whose decoding of print begins at the meaning level instead of the syllable sound level may read synonyms such as "pony" for "horse," or they may read antonyms, night for day. All too often, it can be far worse, and they may utter meaningless "word" nonsense. Mrs. Helen R. Lowe recorded more than 10,000 reading errors she heard in many years of working with students from six to twenty-six, discussed in her 1951 study, <u>How They Read</u>, a copy of which I received years ago from Bettina Rubicam of the former Reading Reform Foundation, Scottsdale, Arizona. Among the errors were Switzerland for Massachusetts, absence for attendance, noodles for mill bells, twelve onions for the travelworn paper bag, and molasses and radishes for masses of reddish gold clouds.

None of those errors could have been made by children who had been taught that syllable sound, not word meaning, is the beginning step in decoding. Added here is an error the writer heard, when testing the oral reading accuracy of a second-grade Scott, Foresman student many years ago. Instead of, "The dog has learned to do..." the child read, "The dog has lemon to do...." The child was totally divorced from the syllable level and was pathetically dependent on the word level, even when she must have known that it made absolutely no sense. That is particularly interesting because she did pass the short "reading comprehension" questions, which suggested she was an intelligent little girl.

DIFFERENT APPROACHES IN TEACHING READING PRODUCE DIFFERENT RESULTS

The previous material, of course, contains no proof that dropping the syllable at the beginning level of learning written speech does make a change in how the brain ultimately processes printed language. Yet there is some historical proof that people taught by syllables initially do read differently from those taught by "words". The proof consists in part by considering three recorded cases of the effects of partial aphasia on the ability to read. These three cases appeared in the time period concerned here, from before 1820 when learning meaningless syllables was the virtually mandatory step in beginning reading in English, to the 20th century, when the sounds of whole words, or just the meanings of whole words, was the initial step.

The oldest recorded case, from before 1828, can be compared to two in the early 20th century. These three cases show marked differences in what appear to be the conditioned reflexes that must have been learned at the very beginning stage of literacy.

Concerning the definition for such partial aphasia, it is not the total loss of speech, but only loss of the ability to read or to write speech. Dr. Hilde L. Mosse wrote of it on page 52 of her text, The Complete Handbook of Reading Disorders, Human Sciences Press, Inc., New York, 1982:

"…damage to certain crucial shunts or sidings [in the brain] invariably causes loss of function. Brodmann's Area in the angular gyrus in the parietal lobes… is such a shunt. Any kind of damage to it causes Alexia (complete inability to read) and at least a partial Agraphia (inability to write.)…."

In order to evaluate these differences in the three partial aphasia cases to be described, it is also helpful to consider the definition for reading given by the 20th century Russian psychologist, D. B. Elkonin, Institute of Psychology, Academy of Educational Science, in his article, "The Psychology of Mastering the Elements of Reading":

"In the present paper, we start from the proposition that reading is a reconstitution of the sound forms of a word on the basis of its graphic representation. Understanding, which

20

is often considered as the basic content of the process of reading arises as a result of correct recreation of the sound forms of words. He who, independently of the level of understanding of words, can correctly recreate their sound forms is able to read." (Page 165, Brian and Joan Simon, Educational Psychology in the U.S.S.R, Stanford University Press, Stanford, California, 1963).

And what must Elkonin's "sound forms of words" be? They must be collections of syllables. It is obvious, of course, that the Russian psychologist Elkonin's definition of reading is about the total opposite of any definition of reading that might have been made by the 20th century American psychologist, E. L. Thorndike.

The earliest recorded case of Alexia, or inability to read, which is available was described by Dr. R. M. N. Crosby, in his book, The Waysiders, Delacorte Press, New York, 1968, page 103. Dr. Crosby wrote of the experience of a British physician in the early nineteenth century, Dr. Lordot. In 1843, Dr. Lordot told of his temporary loss of ability to read in 1825. Before that date, the use of complete syllable tables for beginners, both in America and Great Britain, had been the norm. Children's initial introduction to reading had been divorced, totally divorced, from "meaning" and was concentrated solely on learning how to read printed syllable sounds, followed by learning meaningless but phonically arranged lists of words in spelling books. Therefore, Lordat, who was fully grown when he had his 1825 experience, would have almost certainly learned to read by concentrating initially on syllable sounds in the syllable tables, just as a baby learning to speak babbles syllable sounds. In order to learn to read printed syllables, of course, Dr. Lordat first had to memorize the names and shapes of the 26 letters of the alphabet which form the syllables. Lordat reported in 1843:

"Whilst retaining the significance of words heard, I had lost that of their visible signs. Syntax had disappeared along with words: the alphabet alone was left to me, but the function of the letter for the formation of words was a study yet to be made. When I wished to glance over the book which I was reading when my malady overcame me, I found it impossible to read the title. I shall not speak to you of my despair, you can imagine it. I had to spell out slowly most of the words, and I can tell you, by the way, how much I realized the absurdity of the spelling of our language. After several weeks of profound badness and resignation, I discovered whilst looking from a distance at the back of one of the volumes in my library that I was reading accurately the title Hippocratis Opera. This discovery caused me to shed tears of joy."

Note that his loss of ability to read was total, except for the letters of the alphabet. Isolated letters and other meaning-bearing symbols, such as $ and %, are thought to be stored on the right side of the brain, where the Japanese Kanji meaning-bearing characters are known to be stored. Yet the syllabary, which is pure sound, would have been stored on the left or language side of Dr. Lordot's brain, where the Japanese Kana syllables are known to be stored, and so would the spelling book words which later were built from that sound-bearing syllable foundation.

Note Dr. Lordot's curious comment that "Syntax had disappeared along with words…" He obviously meant syntax in print since he had no loss of spoken syntax. Like the ancient Greeks and Romans, he also had begun as a child by reading only syllables first, so perhaps he had a mind-set like them which we do not.

It was not until about the time of Charlemagne, around 800 A. D., that words were separated in written material. Before about 800 A. D., readers had to separate texts of run-together syllables into words and sentences while they were actually reading, and to do so very quickly. Those syllable-trained readers must have had a well-developed sense of syntax that developed into an actual skill which we lack today, since they had no trouble reading those run-together texts that lacked spaces between words and which lacked even punctuation marks. Perhaps Dr. Lordat shared some of that skill.

Dr. Lordot apparently had a temporary impairment of some sort on the left side of his brain, which affected the area concerned with reading "sound" (presumably the left angular gyrus area, where problems are known to account for alexia). Apparently he had no impairment to its mirrored counterpart on the right side of the brain (presumably a right angular gyrus area), which presumably deals with the "meaning" of symbols like the alphabet and Japanese Kanji characters.

The second case of temporary loss of reading ability was reported on page 32 of <u>Inside the Brain</u> (Dr. William H. Calvin and Dr. George A. Ojemann, A Mentor Book, The New American Library, Inc., New York, 1980). The case concerned a man who would have learned to read about 1915 or so. That was when the syllabary was no longer taught, but when real, sound-bearing "supplemental phonics" was used on whole words. The account stated that:

"…he discovered to his astonishment that he could not read. He could… recognize the letters individually, but only the shortest two- and three letter-words made any sense…."

Teaching of the syllabary had been totally dropped almost a hundred years previously, but the dominant beginning reading method used about 1915 was heavy supplemental sound-bearing phonics and phonically-based spelling books. Therefore, most of that man's reading ability must have been acquired with such sound-based materials. However, beginning phonic reading books in that circa-1915 pro-phonic period did use occasional sight words. After the man lost almost all of his ability to read from his left-brain stroke, he could still read those few short words that he may have learned as a beginning reader by their meaning, not by their sound. Those words and the letters of the alphabet that he had learned by "sight" had to have been stored on the right side of his brain.

22

The third case was reported by Sid J. Segalowitz in <u>Two Sides of the Brain</u>, Prentice Hall, Inc., Englewood Cliffs, New Jersey; 1983, page 92. It concerned a man who obviously showed no syllable-sound retention at all, since he had a massive left-brain stroke that wiped out his ability to speak. After his aphasia which blocked all speech, he still retained a healthy ability to read - but obviously he had to be reading with his right brain. He would have learned in the early 20th century, when sight-words were still massively taught in some few of the schools, the "best" schools, since the "experts" completely endorsed sight words. For instance, the rich and famous Rockefeller children had the "benefit" of the "best" elementary education. As a result, Nelson Rockefeller (who almost became president) was acknowledged to have had great trouble reading. The record suggests Rockefeller was a "functional illiterate". (Concerning the recommendations of the "best" people, see the educational journals published by Columbia Teachers College and the University of Chicago from about 1905 to 1935.) Since the normal right-brain is presumed to have no sound ability, that man's strange case demonstrates that he was reading totally by sight-word "meaning". In all probability, he had been taught, at the beginning level, to do just that.

These three cases of partial aphasia powerfully suggest a difference in the way in which each of these subjects had been taught to read. The pre-1825 case powerfully suggests that the beginning method used to teach reading to that man was the syllabary. The man needed syllable sounds in reading, just as in listening, so he could not read any words at all when the sound side of his brain for reading was blocked. Yet the other two 20th century cases showed partial retentions (in one case) - and almost complete retentions (in the other case) of whole word memories which had to have been stored by "meaning" in their "soundless" right brains after their left- brain strokes. These three cases certainly support the contention that the "syllable" was dropped as the beginning step after 1826, and that "words" became the norm for teaching beginning reading after that date.

Over thirty years ago, some experimental work concerning emotions was based on an interesting, generally unknown fact concerning reading. It was reported in a <u>New York Times</u> article of May 2, 1985, by Daniel Goleman, entitled "Insights Into Self Deception." Besides other sources, the article reported on the experimental work by Richard Davidson, Jonathan Perl and Clifford Saron which was carried out at the State University of New York in Purchase, New York. That group had devised a lens so that words could be read by the right hemisphere of the brain alone or by the left hemisphere of the brain alone. (Obviously, Dr. Lordat could not have been one of their subjects, as he could only handle left-brain print, but these researchers were drawing on a 20th century population which had been taught meaning-bearing words which potentially can be stored on left or right.)

Davidson/Perl/Saron found, and were obviously expecting, that there was a time lag in responding to images of emotionally disturbing, negative words if the words were projected to be read by the right hemisphere, but there was no such time lag if the words were projected to be read by the left hemisphere. The purpose of their research was only to study the presence of such emotional reactions, but it was based on something generally unknown about reading but which they obviously knew, that there is a difference in the way that the right and left hemispheres process print. Since, when using the right hemisphere, the meaning of the words was perceived before the words were spoken, that meant that reading on the right resulted in the use of conscious attention before the words were identified. However, when using the left hemisphere, the words were spoken automatically before the meaning was perceived, which means that reading on the left was done automatically, without the use of consciousness..

Concerning the three cases of partial aphasia which have just been cited, it was only Dr. Lordat, the syllable-trained reader, who used only his left side to read (since he had lost all ability to read words, unlike the other two). Therefore, he was the only one reading automatically, since the other two made some use of the right side, and therefore some consciousness (in one case) - or a great deal of it (in the other case). These results should be compared to the kind of reading reported by the government study cited later, which maintained that all of its present-day subjects read by consciously guessing their way through a text, not automatically identifying the words, as a computer can do, but "psycholinguistically."

THE SLOW SWITCH FROM SOUND TO MEANING EXPLODED IN THE MID 1820'S

The following confirms that the decisive switch from "sound" to "meaning" occurred in 1826 in the the United States, and in the 1820's in England and Scotland.

The beginning reading texts in America before 1826 had been overwhelmingly geared to "sound." Of 48 beginning reading texts in America available to this writer for review whose first editions were published from 1702 to 1825, a clear move from "sound" to "meaning" showed up in only 7 of the 48, and, before 1822, in only 3 of the total to that date. All three of those earliest ones published before 1822 turned out, upon further examination, to have been written by probable change-agents, even though all three authors had a title quite properly revered by conservatives: "Reverend."

The 1802 <u>American Definition Spelling Book,</u> with a clear shift towards "meaning," was written by the Reverend Abner Kneeland. Kneeland's later rather spectacular history and associations are outlined by Samuel L. Blumenfeld on page 94-95 of his text, <u>Is Public Education Necessary? (1981, 1985)</u>, but Kneeland most definitely was an activist as early as 1802, to judge from the nature of the 1802 book.

The second text before 1822 with a sharp move from "sound" to "meaning" is the <u>Pennsylvania Spelling Book</u> of 1815 by "An Association of Teachers". It was copyrighted by Maskell M. Carll and Daniel L. Peck, who were most likely its compilers. So the probable author (or co-author) was the Reverend M. M. Carll, of Philadelphia, whose name appeared later on a publication of the Franklin Institute, Philadelphia, New York Public Library Volume cpv 1262, that establishes that Carll was an activist at that time, but for the establishment of government schools.

Volume cpv 1262 contained "A Report on the State of Education in Pennsylvania, Accompanied with Two Bills for the Establishment of a General System of Public Instruction and Other Proceedings, February 11, 1830." Also "An Address on the Moral and Political Importance of General Education Delivered at the Franklin Institute February 26, 1830, by the Reverend M. M. Carll, Philadelphia, 1830".

As Blumenfeld documented in his book, Is Public Education Necessary ?(1981-1985), the activists A. Bronson Alcott and William Russell were busy visiting Pennsylvania in that same time period, working for the establishment of government schools there. So the Reverend Carll, whose name was involved with one of the three very earliest "meaning" oriented spellers, also had his name show up in Philadelphia associated with a huge drive for government schools that was going on in that circa 1830 time period. With Carll, as with so many other activists of that period, the push for government schools was tied right in with the push for "meaning" and against the syllable in beginning reading.

A text in 1819, The Columbian Spelling Book, which was written by A Friend to Youth, also made a sharp early move from "sound" to "meaning." Its author's signature, A Friend to Youth, had also been used on the 1802 Franklin Primer (which had made a slightly lesser shift to "meaning") and which is attributed to the Reverend Samuel Willard. Since Willard is also credited with writing the watershed 1826 Franklin Primer, his association with activists is very clear, indeed.

In 1826, unlike these three earlier books showing only a partial shift to "meaning," three openly "meaning" oriented beginning readers appeared, and the most important of them was Willard's 1826 Franklin Primer. These three watershed 1826 books will be described later. However, the publication of books like them reached a flood tide shortly after 1826, and "sound" oriented books almost totally disappeared. The change in published materials after 1826 was so quick and so obvious that it is really startling.

The original idea, of course, to move from "syllables" to "words", came from France in 1719 and was used there to some small degree for many years. After the arrival of the French Revolution in 1789, the topics of education, and the teaching of reading, began to be covered in the Convention (the legislature). However, by 1792, the French Revolution had degenerated into a bloodbath. That is why it is astonishing to learn, in the "Bibliographie" of the Dictionnaire de Pedagogie et d'Instruction Primaire (1880-1888), Paris, France, how very many books on education managed to be published in that awful year of 1792, and more than double that in the next year, 1793. Furthermore, many (perhaps almost all) were published by the Convention's own printing press!

From the "Bibliographie," it is obvious the French Convention very much concerned itself with the ideas in these books, such as for "national" education (the shaping of children's minds by the state), compulsory education, government normal schools (the shaping of the minds of the children's teachers by the state), and obviously, reading instruction. While the Revolutionists' big ideas on education were largely mere talk in France during the disordered Revolutionary period, except for the government normal school, the Convention did have that printing press, so these French ideas survived.

It might be said that new and different reading methods which concentrated on "meaning" or on "sound" were conceived in eighteenth-century France, were gestated in the French Revolution, and were ready to be sent out into the world by the beginning of the nineteenth-century, in the very same "Revolutionary" printed package that promoted government schools.

After all, the beginning of the nineteenth century is exactly when the shift from "sound" to "meaning" in the teaching of reading first became apparent in English-language sources, as with Richard Edgeworth's 1798 recommendations in the book he wrote in Ireland jointly with his daughter, Maria, Practical Education. His 1799 A Rational Primer, urged that the ancient syllable method be dropped and be replaced by the study of letter sounds in whole words. That was a pronounced shift to "meaning" and apparently the first such one in the English language.

However, this was also shortly before the time that Edgeworth is known to have been working hard to promote government or national schools in Ireland, as shown later by 1806 correspondence quoted by Andrew Bell. (Some further explanation seems needed with this, as the infamous English Penal Laws, forbidding education to the Catholic Irish, were not repealed until about 1830.) Therefore, Edgeworth's activities demonstrate the twin packaging of government schools and "meaning" instruction for beginning reading, although for Edgeworth with some kind of analytic phonics, but how much is unknown. By doing so, he was jettisoning the almost three-thousand-year-old ABC syllable method.

Andrew Bell is famous as one of the early 19th century promoters of monitorial schools, in which older pupils teach younger ones. He became famous for his school in India, covered in his first book, The Madras School, Elements of Tuition, London, 1808. In it, he also discussed his plan for sharply reducing the oral spelling of the letters in syllables when children were learning words. Yet he still retained some oral spelling.

Omitting the reciting of the names of the letters in the syllables of words that were being learned had been recommended many years before in France by Py Poulain Delaunay in 1719, by Cherrier in 1755, by Viard in 1759, and by Boisjermain in 1778 and in the French Revolution Year VI. However, those writers had recommended the omitting of all spelling or naming of letters in syllables. Bell merely shortened the practice, and wanted learners to recite the letters in a word all at once, but pausing at each syllable (not a bad idea, actually.) That was instead of the former complicated practice of naming the letters in each syllable, and pausing after every new syllable to repeat all the other syllables already named (u-m, um, b-r-e-l, brel, umbrel, l-a la, umbrella.) Nevertheless, Bell was moving away from a greater emphasis on syllables.

Yet by the time that Bell published his 1818 book (since its available 1824 edition is presumably the same as his unavailable 1818 one) he had dropped all oral spelling or naming of letters in new words. Perhaps that had resulted from his contacts with Richard Lovell Edgeworth, which began shortly before his 1808 book was published.

Bell's 1808 book contained a copy of a letter he wrote to Richard Lovell Edgeworth in 1806, and it contained Bell's views at that time on teaching beginning reading and his views on setting up government schools for the "Children of the Poor." In his 1808 book, he also included a "Copy of a letter from Richard Lovell Edgeworth, Esq., dated Oct. - 1806." asking for Bell's further comments on education, so obviously Bell and Edgeworth were sharing ideas. Edgeworth as early as 1798 opposed the teaching of syllables and endorsed the teaching of whole words. By 1818, Bell had joined him. Both men had shared something else: the interest in promoting government schools.

Bell's school in India had used the "monitorial" system, where older students taught younger students, cutting down on the need to employ teachers, therefore making more possible the availability of funds for government schools. Monitorial schools were widely promoted up to the 1840's, but their utility is greatly open to question. (Joseph Lancaster in England and later in America was another famous promoter besides Bell of monitorial schools.)

John Wood of the Edinburgh Sessional School in Scotland, apparently from about 1819, is famous for maintaining a monitorial school. Wood is famous for something else. He totally dropped the "sound"-based syllabary in the teaching of beginning reading, and instead promoted heavy questioning on the sight-word "meaning" of what was read, as will be discussed.

In America, the sudden appearance in 1826 of at least three texts advocating teaching children by sight-word "meaning" instead of "sound," the Franklin, the Worcester, and the Keagy, about the same time as Wood's radical sight-word book in Scotland must have been written, indicates that the sight-word idea, like the idea of government schools, was shared by some common group of people.

The record indicates that the activist group was trans-Atlantic, involving persons in Scotland, England and America. Besides the Scot, John Wood of the Edinburgh Sessional School, the group probably included, among others, Lord Brougham, and Reverend Bell, all Scots who ended up in England, and the Scot Dugald Stewart who had been Brougham's professor at the University of Edinburgh. It included the Welsh-born socialist, Robert Owen, who had worked in England before running a factory in New Lanark, Scotland. It also included his equally activist son, Robert Dale Owen, who became an American after both Owens had failed with their utopian community set up in 1824 in New Harmony, Indiana. The American group included the Scot, William Russell who was editor of the American Journal of Education, which started in 1826, the American Josiah Holbrook and his associates and their American Institute of Instruction which started in

1830, most of the Boston intellectuals named by Samuel Blumenthal in his book, Is Public Education Necessary?, including A. Bronson Alcott, and other American activists named by Blumenfeld.

In America, an unnecessary move to government schools started in Boston in 1818, when its original primary schools were opened, even though that city had excellent private primary education already, as Blumenfeld showed in his text, Is Public Education Necessary?, and had no need for new primary schools.. However, it was not until 1826 that the move to abandon the syllabic "sound" spelling book and to move to "meaning"- bearing sight-words really exploded, when three critical and widely promoted books were published in that same year that openly promoted the "meaning" method.

The first was The Franklin Primer, with an emphasis on word "meaning," instead of syllable "sound," even though it did print a syllable table at the beginning. A Franklin County, Massachusetts, convention of "school committees" had adopted it, and it is presumed to have been written by Reverend Samuel Willard (author of "meaning"- tilted earlier works going back to the 1802 [Benjamin] Franklin Primer). It received great praise from the activist editor of the American Journal of Education, William Russell, in October, 1826, and it had 24 editions by 1840 so it was obviously very widely used after 1826. The later editions of the Franklin Primer continued to publish compliments the material was supposed to have received earlier, such as these:

"These books have also received the approval of a Convention [Ed. the 1826 one in Franklin county] called for the purpose of promoting the cause of Education in Common Schools. This convention was largely attended, and consisted of Teachers and Delegates from five states. Favorably noticed by many of the most distinguished Professors and successful Teachers in New England....."

The Primer was followed shortly after by three other books in the series. Reportedly, in a magazine published in Boston, Liverpool, and London, the series had been praised as the best one in English.

Another printed comment was, "They have been lately reviewed and noticed with approbation in the Revue Encyclopedique (published in the city of Paris) one of the most distinguished Scientific Journals published in Europe...."

Paris? London? Liverpool? Five states? For a child's reading series published in rural Massachusetts? Were the publishers lying about many of the people praising the series? That is very possible. Or are we to think that those far-flung people in Liverpool, London and Paris actually did claim to have read and to have approved the books, as a favor to like-minded contacts, the promoters of this series? Did they approve of the books even though those people never even saw the books? Otherwise, are we supposed to believe that the little four-book finished series was really sent by ship long before 1830 to London and to Liverpool, and to Paris, and that the little books were carefully read by contacts there, who then compared them to other series of readers? Whatever the truth is, mostly lies which is probable, or only part lies, the promotional material published for this series reeks of change-agent activism.

The second critical 1826 beginning book for children was A Primer of the English Language for Parents and Schools by Samuel Worcester, copyright Boston, October 9, 1826, Hillliard, Gray, Little and Wilkins. This completely omitted the syllable tables. There is no question that Worcester meant the book to be a radical change, as he began his "Directions to Teachers" with this sentence: "In order to teach this PRIMER, it will be absolutely essential that the instructor should abandon the common method of teaching children to read and spell."

The third critically important 1826 book is The Pestalozzian Primer, or First Step in Teaching Children the Art of Reading and Thinking, by John M. Keagy, M. D., John S. Wiestling, Harrisburg, Pennsylvania. Keagy wrote a Preface to this book which completely opposed the syllabary and completely endorsed "meaning" in teaching beginning reading, and he worked for years afterwards (and before) to promote those changes. He praised the Pestalozzian approach, which promoted working with real objects, and giving oral lessons instead of assigning written ones. Keagy seemed to be surprisingly sincere and unconnected to most activists, but he was manifestly very wrong.

Keagy wrote in his introduction (page 10):

"After a child has been about two years exercised in a thinking and oral course, he may be taught reading. And here he should not be taught his letters at first, but whole words should be presented to his eyes, after the same manner that some teachers of the deaf and dumb commence the reading business with their pupils. This is the surest method of making them learn to read understandingly. The most familiar words [Ed. Comment: high frequency?] should be given him… It is better not to give him words of more than two syllables. These lessons should be read as if they were Chinese symbols, without paying any attention to the letters, but special regard to the meaning When the child can read whole words with facility, then, and not till then, let him be taught his alphabet, and syllabic spelling… The reason why we have not followed this course in the present work is, that the public is not yet ready for receiving such views with a favorable eye…. Ten or fifteen years hence might be the time.."

At the American Lyceum meeting in 1832, Keagy said (quoted by Mitford Mathews in Teaching to Read, Historically Considered, The University of Chicago Press, 1966, page 65):

"It is in the spelling book that the almost universal habit of reading without thinking is acquired, the tendency of which, says Dugald Stewart, is to abolish the intellectual faculties... The child... should by no means be taught his letters, or spelling at first, but whole words should be presented to him, to be pronounced at sight. This is the surest method of learning to read understandingly and speedily. He should read his lessons as if the words were Chinese symbols... with special regard to the meaning...."

These 19th century "scientific' minds lacked the knowledge we have, today, that reading should be an automatic skill, stored in the automatic sensory-motor portion of the brain. Like all skills that are properly formed (bike riding, brushing the teeth), it can, by definition, be carried out either with complete conscious attention on it or no conscious ("thinking") attention on it. The only way to force conscious attention on reading is to replace automaticity with damaged reading reflexes, which demand the use of consciousness in order to figure out words from the meaning of the context, "psycholinguistically". Unknown to Keagy, who seemed to have very good intentions, what he was actually promoting was the formation of damaged conditioned reflexes. If conscious attention is divided when reading by any need to figure out words, it actually lowers the understanding that Keagy was trying to promote.

Keagy could not have been more in error that the change was ten years away. The wide-open, deliberate, programmed and extraordinarily successful change in beginning reading instruction, from "sound" to "meaning," began in that same year of 1826. That campaign was carried out by the activists who were working (also successfully) to replace America's thriving and successful private education facilities with government schools. The two movements were joined like Siamese twins.

The same general movements as those in America, for a change in reading instruction and for government interference in elementary education, were underfoot in Great Britain, but with the use of different names.

Edgeworth in Ireland dates from 1799, Andrew Bell in England from 1808, but, far worse, from his 1818 (and later) revisions. John Wood's awful primer in Scotland may have dated earlier than its confirmed date of 1828, since his directing of the Edinburgh Sessional School dated at least to 1819. However, his primer was extraordinarily "successful" in the reviews given it (if such harm to children can be called, "successful"). The Wood primer duly showed up on the American side of the water, and was then duly lathered with praise there, also. It completely omitted the syllable tables, taught sight words, and emphasized, to an exhausting and pointless degree, material concerning "meaning."

However, the best way to evaluate John Wood's monitorial school and his primer is to read a book by an anonymous Scottish Schoolmaster, who had spent much time visiting the school and who described what he saw. His book's title was <u>Letters Addressed to the Parochial Schoolmasters of Scotland, Concerning the New Method of Tuition, Containing Strictures on Professor Pillan's Principles of Elementary Teaching</u>, By a Schoolmaster,

Edinburgh: 1829. The book was a collection of letters published between November 30, 1827, and August 15, 1828, with additional material after that. The Schoolmaster was responding to Pillans' remarks vilifying the Church of Scotland Presbyterian parish schools and praising the monitorial schools, which had originally been founded by Andrew Bell and Joseph Lancaster. The Schoolmaster's book is learned, intelligent, amusing, and absolutely devastating in its account of the worthlessness of Wood's Sessional School. One of the letters the Schoolmaster included in his book was from a defender of John Wood's Sessional School, written apparently shortly after November 30, 1827:

"…(the school's) practical results have commended for it the approbation and patronage of such men as Professor Stewart, Brougham, Malthus, and Hume."

Stewart was the famed philosopher from the University of Edinburgh, Brougham a famous member of the English Parliament, and Malthus wrote on populations, but Hume was not the earlier famous Hume. The parochial Schoolmaster responded:

"As to the parade of great names that my opponent brings forward to vouch for the excellence of the new method of teaching, they weigh no more with me than if he had substituted in their stead Shadrach, Meschach, and Abednego; for although Stewart, Brougham, Malthus and Hume be very eminent men in their own vocations, they might nevertheless prove but indifferent schoolmasters."

What those names did, establish, however, was that there was in the 1820's in Great Britain, as in America, a semi-organized movement to make powerful changes in elementary education, and the most visible change was in beginning reading instruction.

Further very concrete, visible proof that the switch did take place - the abandonment of the syllabary after 1826 - is available at one of Harvard's incredible libraries. Harvard's amazing early 19th century textbook collection was apparently largely the result of gifts of used textbooks from families who donated no-longer-used textbooks to the Harvard Library. Those once-used textbooks, of course, are a guide to actual practices in the period in which they were published. When I was enrolled at Harvard for a summer course in 1986, I had access to those incredible libraries and I found it possible to review early 19th century spellers. At that time, they were available in open stacks at Harvard's Gutman library.

There was a marked difference between the pre-1826 and post-1826 spellers. The pre-1826 spellers had tattered - or missing - syllable-table pages. Those were the pages that had to be used first by beginners who were learning the syllable tables. Obviously, they had been very heavily used. However, in the post-1826 spellers, the syllable tables were in pristine condition, and so obviously had not been used. Obviously unused were the partial (and inadequate) syllable tables in the silly little, post-1826, so-called sight word "primers" that had suddenly appeared and just as suddenly (post-1826) replaced Webster's masterpiece speller as the beginning textbook. It is true that Webster's speller did often continue in use above the critical first-grade level after 1826, but by that time the conditioned reflexes in reading would already have been established and so Webster's could no longer produce automaticity in reading.

CONCERNING THE HIGH LEVEL OF LITERACY FROM WEBSTER'S AND OTHER SYLLABLE-BASED METHODS, AND THE OPPOSITION TO THEM

Concrete records are available concerning the success of Webster's speller, and those like it, with little children. What is surprising is that perhaps the best testimony concerning its success came from someone who spent massive efforts trying to remove the Webster speller and those like it. He was one of the change-agents of the period, William Andrus Alcott, an associate of Gallaudet's and of other change-agents of the period. His cousin was A. Bronson Alcott, who went to Pennsylvania about 1830 with William Russell, the Scot activist editor of the <u>American Journal of Education,</u> to work for government schools. (See Samuel Blumenfeld's <u>Is Public Education Necessary</u>? 1981, 1985). In 1840, A. Bronson Alcott paid a visit to England, to mingle with other luminaries there. Earlier, he had run a private school in Boston, but his wealthy clientele abandoned him when he instituted what they considered at that time to be risque curriculum.. He did have a lovely daughter, Louisa May Alcott, who wrote <u>Little Women</u>.

A. Bronson Alcott had a less-well known cousin, the above-mentioned change agent of the period, William Andrus Alcott (1798-1859). William Andrus Alcott wrote a kind of autobiography in 1839, <u>Confessions of a Schoolmaster,</u> published by Gould, Newman and Saxton, Andover, Massachusetts, and New York. In it, he gave his age at different periods, but he did not tie it into dates. However, since his birth date is known, it is easy to tell the actual years in his account.

From the ages of four to eight, William Andrus Alcott attended the "district" school, which is what the village or town schools were called, but at that time there was no state control over the schools. Alcott wrote, "Two summers and one winter had made me a 'speller,' as it was then called, and a tolerable reader of easy lessons." That means, at the age of 5, in 1803, he could both read and spell.

Alcott became a schoolmaster himself, at the age of 18 in 1816, until about 1825. Another book he wrote was <u>Historical Description of the First Public School in Hartford</u> in 1832. This "First Public" school was apparently under some kind of state control, and state control is exactly what the American government activists were promoting at the time. That is because they knew better than we do that Federal, but not state control, is effectively outlawed by our Constitution. That "First Public School" was teaching beginning reading for "meaning", with endless repetition of the same short selections, so that children could concentrate on expression and "meaning". However, Alcott praised the awful practices, and then held up, as scandalous, the following from earlier times:

"A class in a town adjoining this, consisting of two pupils about five years of age, read one day, in my presence, a lesson containing sixty-six different words, of which more than forty were nouns, pronouns, verbs, and adjectives. Now, of these forty words, I suppose these pupils had not the remotest conception of the meaning of more than six or eight. It would be difficult to describe the various positions of the limbs, and contortions of the muscles, especially those of the face, which were observable during the ten minutes in which they were thus obliged to do penance."

This is very interesting testimony from a contemporary witness who observed this some time before 1832, and perhaps some considerable time, since Alcott, himself, had been a teacher for some time. As only one day's lesson, two five-year-olds had the unassisted reading of a list of sixty-six relatively low frequency words (and they must have been low frequency words since Alcott claimed the children did not know the meaning of most of them). Alcott implied the children were able to work out the pronunciation of those words all by themselves, correctly. He also implied that the day's lesson of sixty-six words for the five-year-olds to work out was only one of a sequence of similar lessons for them. The children were obviously reading their way successfully through word lists in a speller like Webster's, and maybe it was Webster's, at the young age of five. Alcott said elsewhere that he, himself, had done that at the age of about five, as already discussed.

Compare that independence in pronouncing print to the sight-word beginning vocabulary of William Scott Gray's "Dick and Jane" Scott, Foresman series. The entire vocabulary of Gray's 1930 material covered in the first six months or so of first grade might equal only one-day's lesson for five-year-olds a century earlier, to sound out all by themselves. Even so, every one of the "Dick and Jane" vocabulary sight-words had to be pronounced by the teacher first because children taught with "Dick and Jane" could not sound out the words first by themselves, as the children a hundred years earlier were able to do.

Alcott was also greatly disapproving in 1832 of the performance of a nine-year-old girl he had seen some time before, and very probably long before. He wrote:

"In an adjoining county, I once heard a little girl only nine years of age, read nearly the whole of two difficult pages in the American Preceptor at a single lesson. She had no classmate, and was accustomed to read lessons as long or nearly as long as this...."

These children might well have been bored. However, from the five-year-olds to the nine-year old, they were not and never would be "functional illiterates."

There is obviously quite a story behind the suppression of the famous Webster speller for beginners, and of its imitators. The movement was certainly in full, public force by 1826, when Noah Webster finally spoke out in public and finally responded to accusations like those from one of his opponents, Lyman Cobb. Lyman Cobb had been one of the earlier activists in 1821 opposing Webster's speller and publishing spellers in public opposition to the famous speller of Noah Webster. In Cobb's 1828 paper, "Critical Review of Mr. Webster's Spelling Book." Cobb quoted that 1826 article by Webster, and part of it is as follows:

"To the Public, New Haven, Connecticut, March, 1826, by Noah Webster

"In order to accomplish their object, it has been expedient to depreciate my work and to charge me with innovation and with introducing a system of orthography and pronunciation in many respects vague and pedantic... Surely, if this is true, if my book is really a bad one, I have been very much deceived; and I have done not only an injury but great and extensive injury to my country."

There was "great and extensive injury" on its way to America, a crippling near-illiteracy for hosts of Americans, but it certainly did not come from great old Noah Webster, who was largely responsible for making America, in its first 50 years, probably the most literate nation that had ever existed on earth. The "great and extensive injury" came from Webster's activist opponents who were expelling the teaching of the syllable tables from beginning reading instruction.

In both the United States and Great Britain, the "meaning" method activists won out only a few years after Webster wrote that pathetic article in 1826. The complete syllabary, along with Noah Webster's original speller in America, were dropped, like the famous hot potato, for beginning readers after 1826. The change from teaching beginners syllable sounds to teaching instead whole word meanings took place in both the United States and Great Britain in an astonishingly brief span of time, which certainly suggests the work of activists instead of the force of normal market factors. Many new textbooks came into print, which activists pushed for adoption in the new government-controlled schools. (The texts were sometimes written by the activists, probably because the possible profits from "official" texts were tantalizing.)

In the United States, private education and local township schools were replaced by the new state-government-controlled education by about 1840. It introduced rigid control from the top, from the state capitals, under which we are still working. (A former superintendent of schools told me that almost every action he took was governed by rules from the state department of education, and that he therefore had very little freedom in running the town's schools.) The actual use of the syllabary for beginning readers - despite the fact that parts of it often appeared in the silly little new primers - was gone before the 1830's. In England, government-approved and government-paid-for textbooks, using word "meaning" and not syllable "sound", were donated to religious schools and others. They produced a rapid drop in the quality of education.

The continued large sales of Webster spellers all through the 19th century could not have been for government schools, because the various and reliable published records of the period clearly show that the government schools were buying sight-word primers. Yet, unless Webster's publishers were lying, its sales all through the 19th century were enormous. Webster speller was apparently largely being sold through general stores, for the use of the general public, not for schools.

With the advent of the "meaning" method to teach beginning reading, the once marvelous spelling efficiency of the public had disappeared. The hallmark of the "meaning" method is that it produces poor spelling. Therefore, those puzzling continued huge sales suggest that the very cheap Webster "speller" was being used by reading-disabled ordinary citizens to look up correct spellings. The great number of post-1826 American "functional" illiterates would have had trouble when trying to write anything. Since the cost of a hard-cover dictionary would not have been in the budgets of many people in those days, Webster's speller for only ten cents or so could have met their needs.

In America before 1826, Webster's spelling book, with a complete syllabary and his fantastic, unparalleled pronunciation guide for spelled words, had been massively used since shortly after its first publication in 1783. There were many other spellers in print but his was the one that was overwhelmingly used. Webster's speller and the others, such as the 1783 Isaiah Thomas edition of the William Perry 1776 speller from Scotland, produced extraordinary literacy levels. Literacy had been the norm for almost all the American population, except for the greatly unfortunate held in slavery in the South. However, Webster's speller and those like it were mercilessly attacked by the new "meaning" emphasis opponents.

The loosely organized trans-Atlantic activists were remarkably successful, although it took longer for government-controlled schools to take over in Great Britain than in the United States. However, it did not take any longer there to ruin British textbooks for the teaching of beginning reading, as a review of some of those available books can show.

However, while the "given" history at least admits that the syllabary was dropped after the 1820's, it also wrongly claims that America used "phonics" (sounds in whole words) in the 19th century. The terrible functional illiteracy of the period is therefore buried by such false reports such as Nila Banton Smith's fake history of reading, apparently written in the early 1930's for her doctorate at Columbia Teachers College while Thorndike and Gates were still there.. Re-arranging her bibliography by publishing dates makes it abundantly clear that effectively she left out 50 critical years of changes (roughly, from 1840 to 1890). It is almost impossible to see how she could have done that except deliberately in order to hide the true reading instruction history of those years, when several phonic programs had become widely known and in use, before they were buried by a new wave of "reading experts."

In the late 18th and early 19th century, many writers disapproved of having the lower classes literate. Even among those who did promote simple literacy for the lower classes, which lower classes were most probably the great bulk of their populations, many opposed the teaching of handwriting, because, as these activists were perfectly willing to admit, that gave too much power to the lower classes. This writer's text, The History of Beginning Reading, cites multiple examples of such 18th and 19th century anti-literacy positions.

Could the constant promotion for over 200 years of the literacy-crippling "meaning" method and the constant opposition to the literacy-promoting "sound" method have had something to do with the fact that true literacy gives too much power to the general population, which might therefore be more difficult to control? The desire to control populations was the reason that it was illegal to teach slaves to read in some states in the American South before the Civil War. The infamous Penal Laws made it illegal to teach Irish Catholics to read in Ireland from the late 1690's until about 1830. Therefore, the deliberate suppression of literacy in order to control subject populations is actually an historical fact, not just a supposition.

A COMPARISON OF CULTURAL CHANGES, BEFORE AND AFTER THE SYLLABLE METHOD WAS DROPPED

By now, the question needing an informed answer that was mentioned at the beginning of this paper has probably become very obvious. It is, of course, "What was the watershed and enormously harmful change which has been misunderstood and ignored for so very long, for some 200 years?"

The answer, of course, is that the culture-destroying change was the dropping and ignoring of the syllable in the teaching of beginning reading. Yet that change and the problems resulting from that change are virtually ignored to this very day, even though it appeared so long ago, in the early 19th century in the English-speaking world. However, does an actual comparison of "then" with "after" demonstrate that the change was, indeed, catastrophic? To demonstrate that it was, indeed, catastrophic, consider the following confirming facts.

Meaning-trained readers cannot "hear" the printed page with the automatic ease with which they can hear the spoken word. Growth in vocabulary (and complex syntax) largely develops with exposure to written texts, not spoken ones. Failing heavy exposure to reading, people's vocabularies grow more slowly. One of the results is that a different kind of population, one with lower vocabulary levels and with less skill in handling complex syntax is now buying printed materials. The market has reacted to that by producing materials with sharply lower readability levels than were current in the time of George Washington.

"Readability" levels rise or fall as lower-frequency, multi-syllable words increase or decrease. The levels rise or fall as sentences become longer or shorter, which means as syntax becomes more or less complex. The readability levels in ordinary writing (newspapers, books, and personal letters) were far higher before 1826 than afterwards. They dropped after 1826 when the "meaning" method took over in the teaching of beginning reading. However, readability levels took an absolutely plummeting further drop after the arrival of the deaf-mute-method Dick and Jane readers in 1930.

Concerning the enormous drop in readability levels after the 1930 arrival of the pure deaf-mute method in the teaching of reading, consider silent movies before 1927, when the dialog was only in print on the screen, and not spoken. The first movie that ever had any sound at all was the <u>Jazz Singer</u>, in 1927, with Al Jolson's wonderful singing. But, unlike its songs which could be heard because of the new sound track, its dialog was still just silently written on the screen, not spoken. Here is one of its dialog screens:

"Grief, stalking the world, had paused at the house of Rabinowitz."

Consider the complex structure of this purely allegorical sentence, with its low frequency words (stalking, grief, paused, Rabinowitz). The movie magnates (unlike today), made movies only to sell tickets - to make money. They knew that if the audiences could not read and understand the movies' printed dialog, the audiences would stop buying tickets. Yet this movie, The Jazz Singer, was one of the most successful movies of all time, so it is likely that most of the audiences could read and understand the above complex sentence. Yet, just try asking average high school students today to spell the words above - or even to read them, without any context to help with guessing..

Confirmation of such present-day disabilities from the deaf-mute guessing method appears on page 11 of <u>Becoming a Nation of Readers, The Report of the Commission on Reading</u>, The National Institute of Education, U. S. Department of Education, Washington, D. C., 1985:

"...the generally accepted current model of word identification [is that] a possible interpretation of a word usually begins forming in the mind as soon as even partial information has been gleaned about the letters in the word.... When enough evidence from the letters and the context becomes available, the possible interpretation becomes a positive identification."

This model, using context and conscious guessing for word identification, which is based on actual tests on American readers, implies that automaticity is lacking for these readers, not just on unfamiliar words, but on almost ALL words! Computers can read print automatically with almost flawless accuracy and speed. Furthermore, truly competent, rapid, and automatic, reading can be done by people reading aloud in foreign languages of which they have no understanding, when context guessing is therefore impossible. Yet, this awful statement confirms that the American readers they tested can only read print by the use of conscious guessing!

A further statement on page 12 of <u>Becoming a Nation of Readers</u> is that those present-day readers tested do not work out pronunciations by "letters and sounds" but by "analogy with known words," which is the relatively slow, jig-saw-puzzle, two-step deaf-mute skill. So Arthur I. Gates' "intrinsic phonics" is certainly alive and well in America!

The report said further that fourth graders made almost no mistakes with pseudowords such as tob and jate, but that is not consoling, since the report states they had to draw on their sight-word memory bank for similar whole words in order to sound out these simplest of sound sequences - once again, jig-saw-puzzle phonics. They made no use of real, letter-based phonics. Of course, that was no accident, as they were doing just what they had been taught to do by the criminally defective present-day "reading instruction."

Those 20th century defects in reading ability were unknown in the syllable-conscious 18th century. One testimony concerning the 18th century high standards came from someone who later became president of the United States. Surely, he should be considered a reliable source. It was John Adams who wrote in 1765, quoted by John W. Whitehead in Parents' Rights, Crossway Books, Westchester, Illinois, 1985, from Works of John Adams, Charles Adams III, Ed., Boston, 1851:

"(A) native of America who cannot read or write is as rare an appearance... as a comet or an earthquake."

Who could know more about the status of literacy in America than John Adams who lived in America then? Obviously, he never had to be concerned about "functional illiteracy," because it did not exist back then. Of course, Adams was referring to free Americans. Many of the Southern states had appalling laws forbidding the teaching of literacy to slaves, the same kind of literacy-forbidding Penal Laws that were then active in Ireland. All such legislation, of course, has a single and very obvious purpose: to keep subject populations under political control.

The French founder of the famous American family, the du Ponts, Pierre Samuel du Pont de Nemours,(1739-1817) who knew Jefferson personally, wrote in 1800:

"Almost all of the young Americans learn to read, to write and to compute. There are not more than four in a thousand who cannot write legibly and properly"

That obviously met with freedom-loving Jefferson's approval. The comment appeared in du Pont's book, National Education in the United States (160 pages) which was published in France in 1812, and apparently also in Annales de l'Education, M. F. Guizot, Editor, France, 1812. His book began with the statement, "This was made in 1800 at the request of Mr. Jefferson, President of the United States of America; it has the approval of this great judge and of his respectable successor." (For sources on this material, see the du Pont biography in Dictionnaire de Pedagogie et d'Instruction Primaire (1880-1888), Paris, France, Vol. 1 - 1, pages 748 and following, and also entries on du Pont in the Dictionnaire sections, "Bibliography" and "Lecture").

The Federalist Papers, which today are considered very heavy reading, were published in the late 18th century and they were intended for the general population, a population which had learned to read with the syllable "sound" method. Yet nothing published today, with such very heavy reading, would ever be aimed at our general population which was taught to read by the word "meaning" method.

As another example of the decrease in literacy levels, consider the high readability level of ordinary newspapers in the pre-1826 era, and they were bought by the general population. A story in a child's school reader, meant only to be an amusing comment on a familiar failing, implicitly demonstrated how large the reading public was at that time when most of America was rural.

In Clifton Johnson's Old-Time Schools and School-Books, The Macmillan Company, 1904, and Peter Smith, New York, 1935, pages 298-299, a quotation is included from The Monitorial Reader by someone named "Adams," listed as published in Concord, New Hampshire in 1839. (This is not the 1831 Monitorial Primer by J. A. Prest.) Since the selection concerned adults with half-grown children by 1839 or possibly before, the adults would all have learned to read at least 13 years before, which means before 1826, the critical date after which syllable "sound" was dropped in beginning reading. Part of Johnson's long selection reads:

"After all, the lowest, the most degraded class of borrowers are NEWSPAPER BORROWERS; fellows who have not soul enough to subscribe to a newspaper, yet long to know its contents, who watch with lynx-eyed vigilance for the arrival of the mail, and when their more generous neighbor receives his paper, send their boys with messages like the following:

"Mr. Borrowall wishes you would be kind enough to (give) him your paper for one minute. There is something particular in it, that he wants to see; he'll send it back before you want to read it."

Yet "reading expert" ignoramuses in the 1920's claimed illiteracy was widespread in America in the early 1800's, before the government schools took over.

Concerning the level of literacy in 18th century England, a continental visitor to England in 1726 is reported to have said:

"All Englishmen are great newsmongers. Workmen habitually begin the day by going to coffee-rooms in order to read the latest news. I have often seen shoe-blacks and persons of that class club together to purchase a farthing newspaper. (Quoted by Professor Lawrence Stone of Princeton in "Literacy and Education in England" 1640-1900, Past and Present, Number 42, 1969, Oxford, England.)

Literacy among the poor in England was so widespread in the 18th century that Hannah More (1743-1833), a writer of children's books, thought that it was necessary to start her own publishing of cheap penny books to counter what she thought was the harmful content of the widespread penny books, which had such content as "speculative infidelity." More obviously was not worried about the "reading comprehension level" of the largely unschooled poor, since she thought they had the "capacities" to absorb those written arguments for "speculative infidelity"! She lived in the class-conscious England of the 18th century, when the more fortunate often looked down on those less fortunate. She made a remark to Zachary Macaulay in 1796 that confirms the high level of literacy among the poor at that time and for some time before.

"Vulgar and indecent penny books were always common, but speculative infidelity, brought down to the pockets and capacities of the poor, forms a new era in our history."

Hannah More is quoted by Mary F. Thwaite in Thwaite's 1962 and 1973 text, From Primer to Pleasure in Reading, The Horn Book, Inc., Boston, Massachusetts. Thwaite commented concerning Hannah More,

"…it was chiefly due to her that the series of Cheap Repository Tracts was launched. These productions imitated the chapbooks in appearance and price (necessary features if they were to rival them on the market)…. The project, launched in March 1795, was amazingly successful, 300,000 copies of the tracts being sold in the first six weeks, and two million within a year…. Over a hundred were published by 1798, when the series came to an end…. There was no intention of educating poor people or their children beyond their station….."

So, in 1796, the Cheap Repository Tracts were only meant to "rival" the "Vulgar and indecent penny books that were always common…" Since the printing of that "rival" publication, the Cheap Repository Tracts, resulted in producing and selling 2,000,000 copies in a single year, many of those other "always common" and "rival" "penny books" must also have been produced and sold in that very same year. Chapbooks had probably been produced in large numbers for a great many years before 1796, since the chapbook's advent about 1700. It is obvious that the published and purchased numbers of such cheap materials by 1796, for a very much lower population than later, must have been massive. Hannah More made it obvious that the poor, the lower classes, had been buying a large number of those materials before her own materials came on the market in 1795, so the lower classes must have largely been literate. It should also be remembered that, at that time, in England and in the United States, there was no such thing as true government schools, so it was not government schools that produced what was very widespread literacy in England and America in 1796.

For a comparison in published totals, the famous child's book, Alice in Wonderland, was published in England in 1865. From its publication date to 1898, it sold only 180,000 copies in 33 years (reported by Alec Ellis in A History of Children's Reading and Literature, Pergamon Press, Oxford: 1968, page 66.) Admittedly, Alice in Wonderland was a more expensive hard-cover book, and the cheap chapbooks were more like pamphlets, but that is still a staggering drop in comparative sales: from 2,000,000 copies of a chapbook-like edition that were sold in a single year in 1796, to 180,000 copies of a very famous hard cover book in the 33 years up to 1898.

In 1796, no government schools had existed, but in those 33 years of sales for <u>Alice in Wonderland</u> from 1865 to 1898, government-supported schools had been in existence in England. Government-supported schools (both in England and America) date in general from about the early 1820's, and they share another similarity. Both replaced the spelling book, which began with the complete syllabary, with so-called "primers", which were not the real, ancient, religious primers. They were only meant to be the book with which children were taught to read. Those texts minimalized or completely replaced the ancient sound-bearing syllabary, and instead taught with whole words and an emphasis on "meaning."

So, a watershed change took place after the early 1820's. Before the advent of government-supported schools, the syllabary had been used to teach reading, and literacy was widespread. After the government-supported schools arrived, the syllabary was no longer used to teach reading, and illiteracy became widespread.

.The enormous sales of cheap literature in the 18th century confirm that literacy was widespread in England when the syllable method was the way to teach reading. After the word method replaced the syllable method in the 19th century, a huge drop in literacy is confirmed by government-administered literacy tests in England.

Government tests in reading first arrived in England with their Revised Code of 1861, as a trade-in, apparently, for dropping the previous control of government-funded and government controlled textbooks, which had been used in religious and other schools. The reading failures the tests disclosed from those formerly government-approved textbooks were enormous. The 1870 tests demonstrated that the government-controlled schools by 1870 were failing in the most fundamental task, the teaching of reading, as shown by Ellis's comment on page 89 of his text:

"In 1870 the most expected of working-class children by the government was that they should read a newspaper on leaving standard VI, a requirement which could well have been met by a child of 8 years old. Inspectors admitted that no attainment below Standard IV could be of permanent benefit to a child, and yet 80% of children passed only in the lower standards before leaving school."

When children did pass at the lower levels on the 1870 graded tests of reading ability in England known as the Standards, it was largely meaningless, as they were tested on reading books which their classes had read aloud so much that the pages had actually been memorized. A government inspector in Wales in the 1870's said a child could go on "reading" aloud even if the textbook fell on the ground. (From E. M. Sneyd-Kynnersley's autobiography, cited by Pamela Horn in The Victorian Country Child, The Roundwood Press, Kinneton, 1974, Sutton Publishing, Gloucestershire, England.)

Therefore, the "inspectors" who were actually testing the children said that 80% of them in 1870 had received NO benefit from attending the government-controlled schools which were attempting to teach reading, and could not even read a newspaper! That was not only an enormous waste of time and money, but it demonstrated that the government-controlled schools were producing a vast population of 19th century "functional illiterates," a sorry contrast to the vast population of true literates who had lived in England in the government-school-free 18th century, when even bootblacks read newspapers and joined together to buy them. Textbooks for reading instruction, published after the 1820's, make it clear that the ancient syllable method for beginners had been dropped.

However, is there any proof, before government interference with education had begun, that non-governmental education had been generally available in England and America, and that it had used the syllable method to teach literacy? Fortunately, there is a wide body of eighteenth-century literary sources containing clear references to the wide availability of non-governmental teaching of basic literacy, both in England and America.

In America, a high level of literacy cannot be doubted, from the testimony quoted previously from John Adams, and from the testimony of the French founder of the American du Pont family, who discussed literacy and education at great length with no less a personage than Thomas Jefferson! Since the great majority of American beginners were given Webster's spelling book, there cannot be any reasonable doubt that they did begin with the syllable tables!

Concerning England, a famous source confirming the easy availability of beginning reading instruction is the 1765 tale, The History of Little Goody Two Shoes. It was published by the famous John Newbery in London and was technically written by "Anonymous" but is routinely credited to the equally famous Oliver Goldsmith. Little Goody Two Shoes replaced a village dame-school matron who had taught beginners to read, and who was retiring. The tale explains Goody's charming teaching, starting with the syllabary, and concludes with a "happily ever after" ending for Goody. What it does accidentally is to establish that such dame schools were everyday, taken-for-granted institutions in 18th century England, and that the use of the syllabary as the beginning step was so normal that it needed no explanation. At that time, beginning reading in English was taught only by the syllabary, and the horn book (a simple syllabary and the Lord's Prayer, covered with see-through 41 horn) was in wide use as the "textbook.".

Such 18th century village dame schools in England were omnipresent and highly regarded. They left a mark in such things as largely laudatory and anecdotal poetry. Yet, by the mid-19th century, dame schools in England were described with contempt. They had been drummed out of existence by the government schools proponents who had rejected teaching by the syllabary.

Goody Two Shoes is not the only English narrative confirming the importance of dame schools. Mary F. Thwaite (page 152 of her text) recorded another eighteenth-century story concerning the teaching of rural children:

"An interesting example describing a rural dame school of the period is The Village School (ca. 1783) by Dorothy Kilner. Here Mrs. Bell, 'a very good woman', teaches little boys and girls to read…. The clergyman, Mr. Right, is much in evidence. He helps to pay for the poor children's schooling…"

Elwood P. Cubberley included a section, "The English Dame Schools," in his book, Readings in the History of Education (pages 374-377), Houghton Mifflin Company, Boston… 1920. Cubberley quoted poetry written during the period of the dame schools. Concerning such poetry by the Reverend George Crabbe (1754-1832), Cubberly said:

"The English poet Crabbe was essentially a poet of the homely life of the people. In his description of the Borough, in speaking of the "Poor and their Dwellings," he pays a passing tribute of respect and gratitude to his first teacher, in the following lines describing the Dame School he attended:

"'…Shall I not think what pains the matron took,
When first I trembled o'er the gilded book?
How she, all patient, both at eve and morn
Her needle pointed at the guarding horn,
And how she soothed me, when with study sad
I labored on to reach the final zad?…'."

Cubberley quoted all of the long poem. He also said, "Another English poet, Henry White (1758-1806) also describes his school in a somewhat similar vein:"

.

"'In Yonder cot, along whose mouldering walls
In many a fold the mantling woodbine falls,
The village matron kept her little school.
Gentle of heart, yet knowing well to rule…'."

Cubberley also quoted that poem at length, but only a short portion of a third one by William Shenstone (1714-1763), which he said had 350 lines. It was entitled "The Schoolmistress", and was about Shenstone's early dame school teacher. It had appeared in full in Barnard's <u>American Journal of Education,</u> Vol. III, pp. 449-455. It is the opening of the second verse that establishes the omnipresence of the literacy-teaching dame schools in 18th century England:

"In every village mark'd with little spire,
Embowered in trees, and hardly known to fame,
There dwells, in lowly shed and mean attire,
A matron old, whom we schoolmistress name......"

Historically speaking, one of the best sources for reliable facts about a culture are those facts which are mindlessly embedded in the background of its stories and poems. Using this concept as an historical yardstick, it is reasonable to assume that the 18th century dame schools were, generally speaking, pleasant for the students, successful in their teaching, and regarded with respect by the 18th-century public. They were also turning out the great numbers of middle- and lower-class literates who were buying the 18th century massive production of chapbooks in England. Apparently, although cities such as Manchester and Birmingham lacked such "dame schools" and may (or may not) have had high illiteracy rates, most of the population was rural, with "every village mark'd with little spire" having a "schoolmistress."

Teaching beginning reading by the word "meaning" method is difficult and takes years to complete, and it all too often fails, no matter how much time is spent in attempting to teach it. Yet teaching by the syllable "sound" method (particularly if joined with Pascal-type names for the letters) is exceedingly easy and can be done in a few months. The ease of teaching by the syllable method is the reason that literacy in the eighteenth century, before the easy-to-use syllable "sound" method had been dropped for the word "meaning" method, had been far, far more widespread in the English language than is usually reported. The massive statistical proof from the huge numbers of 18th century published materials does confirm the high level of literacy.

The cultural damage from today's literacy defects has never been properly acknowledged. For instance, in the past, many Christian families - as in Dickens' Christmas Carol - gathered around the Bible as portions of it were read aloud. How many families today are literate enough to read the Bible aloud accurately?

Concerning such accuracy in reading: The great majority of those who learn to read by the "sound" method read at an accuracy level of 97 to 100%. When I did my sabbatical research in 1977, I took with me a portion of Psalm 104, Verses 10 to 18, in five different languages, which I had received, at my request, from the gracious American Bible

Society. I only had the opportunity to test Dutch and Swedish sixth-graders with that short selection, and they were chosen at random from their classes. The Swedish teacher commented that the Swedish copy was a very archaic translation, but the children had no trouble reading it. For three Dutch sixth grades, (59 students), 97 % read it at 94% accuracy or above, 88% read it at 97% accuracy or above, and 61% read it at 99 or 100% accuracy, a large majority. For six Swedish sixth grades (56 students), 100% read it at 94% accuracy or above, 93% read it at 97% accuracy or above, and 73% read it at 99 or 100% accuracy, an even larger majority.

In the United States today, most people learned to read by the "meaning" method. Listen to anything read aloud today. It will usually sound very smooth, if the reader felt secure enough about his reading ability to be willing to read aloud, but, if the listener has a copy of the same text, he will usually find it is read at considerably below 100% accuracy - most commonly at about 95%. That is because the speaker is reading the text <u>by</u> its meaning, and not <u>by</u> its sound. The government study of American adults cited earlier demonstrated that those adults were consciously guessing their way down the page from the meaning of its context. They were not "hearing" the print automatically first, and only afterwards getting its meaning, which is true when we are listening to speech, and should be true when we are reading.

The "reading experts" have had their way, unfortunately, since 1930, so that most of us are not reading automatically and effortlessly, as a computer reads, but are instead hard-working "psycholinguistic guessers." Therefore, far too many of us actively dislike reading.

Our impoverished curriculum, particularly in history, largely exists because students cannot handle demanding texts. Now even our country's history is quite literally, a closed book for great numbers of people. That is very dangerous, as ignorant people are targets for harmful propaganda since they lack the knowledge to reject it.

Truly, the move from syllable "sound" to word "meaning" in teaching beginners to read has had terrible results.

It is hardly surprising that the syllable method has had some very historically important personages promoting it. They include the famous Roman educator, Quintilian, from the first century A. D., and Denis Diderot, who was the editor of the famous 18th century <u>Encyclopedie ou Dictionnaire Raissonnee des Sciences, des Arts, et des Metiers.</u>, Paris, France.

The <u>Encyclopedie</u> was published by Denis Diderot, et al, in 28 volumes from 1751 to 1772. An article, "Syllabaire", is on pages 1713-1715 of the S volume. The "Syllabaire" article was probably written by Diderot, himself. It endorsed Pascal-invented phonics that had been in the <u>Grammaire</u> of Port Royal, France in 1664. Blaise Pascal phonics is simply renaming the letters of the alphabet with their apparent sound, instead of their names, so that the syllables and words they form are self-evident. For instance, instead of spelling "see aye tee CAT", a child could recite "cuh - ah - tuh CAT." Pascal letter names suggest the word or syllable produced by them, while letter names may not.

It was probably Diderot himself who wrote the following: "But I shall remark, as an important thing concerning the syllables of which I have indicated the detail and the divisions, it is necessary not to omit a single one in the tables that will be made from them. 'Syllabis nullum compendium est, perdiscendae omnes.' [Ed.: "For learning of syllables there is no short way. They must all be learned through out.") This is the opinion of Quintilian (Inst. I. I. 30) & he wished that one stop the children there until one had all the certitude possible that they were not puzzled in the distinction of a single syllable."

However, Quintilian not only insisted on the importance of teaching the syllables, but he described what happens if they are not taught, producing a condition akin to what today we might label functional illiteracy. To quote him more fully, he wrote in Institutio Oratoria (I. I. 30):

"For learning syllables there is no short way; they must all be learned throughout, nor are the most difficult of them, as is the general practice to be postponed, that children may be at a loss, forsooth, in writing words. Moreover, we must not even trust to the first learning by heart; it will be better to have syllables repeated and to impress them long upon the memory; and in reading, too, not to hurry on, in order to make it continuous or quick, until the clear and certain connection of the letters become familiar, without at least any necessity to stop for recollection. Let the pupil then begin to form words from syllables, and to join phrases together from words. It is incredible how much retardation is caused to reading by haste; for hence arise hesitation, interruption, and repetition, as children attempt more than they can manage, and then after making mistakes, they become distrustful even of what they know. Let reading, therefore, be at first sure, then continuous, and for a long time slow, until by exercise a correct quickness is gained."

Quintilian said the most difficult of the syllables should not be postponed, obviously meaning they should be taught before meaningful texts are used. Applying his recommendation to the period of the Webster speller, it can be seen that Webster followed that recommendation, and did it to handle the multiple differences in English spellings of syllables. Most of the more difficult syllable spellings were automatically handled by their inclusions in Webster's carefully constructed word lists, before his very first, meaning-bearing sentence arrived, far into Webster's speller. That very first sentence was, "No man may put off the law of God." In today's government schools, that sentence would never get past its censors.

Syllables are, indeed, the beginning and irreplaceable step in both spoken and written language and the organized war against their use in teaching beginning reading, some 200 years ago, was, indeed a catastrophic event. That was demonstrated by the collapse of what had been the very general literacy in the English-speaking world of the 18th century, and its replacement by rampant near functional illiteracy ever since.

We should repair that damage in today's world by insisting that beginners are initially taught to read by the sounds of syllables in the ancient syllable table, and then by the sounds of syllables in carefully constructed English word lists, as in the fantastic Webster speller. Then today's children will grow up to read as well as those pre-1826 children whose heavy use produced the tattered and sometimes worn-out syllable tables on the pre-1826 spellers now on the shelves of Harvard's library.

Reading automatically, like those pre-1826 children, instead of "psycholinguistically guessing," today's children can then grow up to find publications like <u>The Federalist Papers</u> as easy to read as <u>The New York Daily News</u>.

APPENDIX A

Concerning the William Scott Gray Reading Tests of 1917
And Later Testing of Oral Reading Accuracy

William Scott Gray (1885-1960) was the author of the watershed 1930 "Dick and Jane" Scott Foresman readers. Edward L. Thorndike (1874-1950) was America's most prominent and highly influential education psychologist from about 1910 until his death in 1950. The work of Gray and Thorndike, and the work of their compatriots, was destined to have an enormous, negative impact on American education and to alter completely the teaching of beginning reading. The reading tests those two men constructed in 1913-1914 can be used as convenient markers for the beginning of that change. However, ever since the 1860's, the "psychologicial" winds blowing over America from such places as Wundt's laboratory in Leipzig, Germany also had an enormous and related influence (See The Leipzig Connection, by Lance J. Klass, with Paolo Lionni, 1979).

In 1913-1914, William Scott Gray constructed his oral reading tests while he was a Columbia Teachers College, New York, master's degree graduate student, under Professor Edward L. Thorndike. At that same time, Thorndike was constructing his first silent reading comprehension tests.

Gray's original 1914 oral reading accuracy tests were somewhat altered over the next two years and were used in testing programs in various city schools. His later revision which follows was part of Gray's 1916 doctoral thesis at the University of Chicago, where Gray remained as a professor until about 1945. Gray's 1916 thesis was reprinted as part of Studies of Elementary School Reading, Supplementary Educational Monographs of the University of Chicago, 1917. It is from that publication that the following reproduced paragraphs and scores for oral testing were taken.

It was presumably in 1916, by which time all 20 of the following revised test paragraphs had apparently become available, that the following oral reading accuracy tests were given, but Gray gave no specific date for the testing. Gray wrote:

"To whom the test was given. - The test was given to 565 pupils from the third to the eighth grade inclusive. These pupils represented four schools, three in the city of New

York and one in a small city in central Illinois. Two of the schools of New York are located in foreign districts of the city. The third New York school represents a more truly American population, economically independent. The Illinois school represents an American population of average economic rank. The pupils were about equally divided between native American and foreign-born children, and represent practically every economic level."

Most paragraphs were four lines long. The paragraphs approximated 60 words for the first five paragraphs (actually 57, 60, 62, 61, and 61 words) and somewhat less as the words in the paragraphs got longer. Gray graded the scores for each paragraph on four increasing levels of difficulty. The Standards ranged from lower expectations to higher expectations. The levels of passing scores for each paragraph were as follows:

At Standard I, four or fewer errors were passing.
At Standard II, three or fewer errors were passing.
At Standard III, two or fewer errors were passing.
At Standard IV, one error or less was passing.

Since the first five paragraphs contained about 60 words, four or fewer errors at Standard I represented about a 93% passing score. That "frustration" level was very possibly based on the level for introducing new words in the deaf-mute teacher Thomas Hopkins Gallaudet's 1835 The Mother's Primer, written for both deaf and hearing children. In his book, The New Illiterates, Samuel L. Blumenfeld concluded that Gray's teaching method in his 1930 Dick and Jane series was most probably based on Gallaudet's 1835 text. Gallaudet was famous, of course, for having founded in 1817 the first successful school for deaf-mutes in the United States.

In the 1835 Gallaudet text, already known words make up about 90% of each new selection. Gallaudet must have concluded that 90% was a large-enough known context for a deaf-mute child to be able guess the meaning of an unknown word embedded in a known context. A child could then remember, solely by its meaning with no sound involved, the visual form of that new word whose meaning he had context-guessed. It is really intriguing that Gallaudet specifically wrote The Mother's Primer for ALL children, not just for deaf-mute children. Therefore, Gallaudet must have wanted children with normal hearing to be taught by the context-guessing, soundless deaf-mute method used in The Mother's Primer.

Yet no mention was ever made by Gray in his 1916 thesis (or ever, so far as is known) of Gallaudet's work, even though Gray's famous 1930 Scott, Foresman reading series was clearly using what must be a deaf-mute method for teaching reading (a controlled vocabulary of already learned sight words, the guessing of new sight words from the meaning of the context, comparison of new sight-words to parts of known sight words to aid in telling them apart, and the carefully calculated repetition of new sight words to fix them in memory).

Gray also computed speed of reading scores. No time limit was required for passing at the above listed accuracy levels. However, rapid reading permitted more errors, as shown below. The "reading experts" had been working on speed of reading for a long time and considered it important.

For Standard I, if read in less than 40 seconds, six errors were permitted, instead of four.
For Standard II, if read in less than 30 seconds, four errors were permitted, instead of three.
For Standard III, if read in less than 25 seconds, three errors were permitted, instead of two.
For Standard IV, if read in less than 20 seconds, two errors were permitted, instead of one.

Gray gave no statistics and no clue, so far as can be learned, concerning how many of those tested were rapid readers. Readers who made four or less errors automatically passed, no matter what their speed, and some of those best readers must have been rapid readers. It was only for those who made more errors that reading rapidly became an advantage in Gray's scoring.

The presumption is made that the reading of these paragraphs at 40, 30, 25, or 20 seconds, or less by grammar school children would informally be considered to be fairly rapid reading. Therefore, the presumption is necessarily also made in reading Gray's results that rapid reading, for those making more errors than others, was in the minority and did not strongly influence his scores. In 1977-1978, the writer tested the oral reading accuracy of about 900 second-grade students in this country and Europe, in their own languages. Rapid reading for inaccurate readers was almost never seen. Inaccurate reading was almost always markedly slower reading.

Following is Gray's total statistical table for his sixth grade scores. The last sixth grade box is an average of all sixth grade Standard scores. Then, the final box is an average for all grades tested, 3 to 6, for all Standards. Weird and almost meaningless as such as an "average" is, a mixing together of all the Standard averages, it nevertheless shows high averages for all grades.

Reproduced separately in the following illustrations, for ease of reference, are the sixth grade Standard I scores. What becomes evident, from the fact that all sixth-graders passed on paragraphs 1 and 2, is that there were no illiterate sixth grade students. Foreign background and the rest, they would all have scored above the so-called "frustration level" on a so-called "reading comprehension" test today, if the content were simple enough. It becomes obvious that New York and Chicago schools were very different in 1916 than they are now. It would be of great interest to repeat that simple Standard I testing of oral reading accuracy in today's schools, but no such simple testing is ever done.

Following are copies of the 20 short paragraphs used in Gray's 1916 testing, and copies of his test results.

1

It was time for winter to come. The little birds had all gone far away. They were afraid of the cold. There was no green grass in the fields, and there were no pretty flowers in the gardens. Many of the trees had dropped all their leaves. Cold winter with its snow and ice was coming soon.

2

Once there lived a king and queen in a large palace. But the king and queen were not happy. There were no little children in the house or garden. One day they found a poor little boy and girl at their door. They took them into the palace and made them their own. The king and queen were then happy.

3

Once a green little leaf was heard to sigh and cry, as leaves often do when a gentle wind blows. "What is the matter, Little Leaf?" said the twig. The little leaf replied, "The wind just told me that one day it would pull me off and throw me down to the ground to die. That is why I am so sad."

4

Once I went home from the city for a summer's rest. I took my gun for a stroll in the woods where I had shot many squirrels. I put my gun against a tree and lay down upon the leaves. Soon I was fast asleep, dreaming of a group of merry, laughing children running and playing about me on all sides.

5

One of the most interesting birds which ever lived in my bird-room was a blue jay named Jakie. He was full of business from morning till night, scarcely ever still. He had been stolen from a nest long before he could fly, and he was reared in a house long before he had been given to me as a pet.

6

Henry was a busy farmer. His farmhouse stood on a hillside above the seashore. Along the shore and up the hillside were the houses of his friendly neighbors. Around his house the ground was flat, like the top of a huge step in the hillside. All about him stretched his small, verdant rice fields.

7

It was a glad summer morning. Little birds teetered on the twigs of the trees. They opened their throats and sang as loud as they could. Flowers nodded to each other in the gardens and along the wayside. Butterflies went flitting about gayly, the morning air was fresh and sweet, and all was gladness.

8

I remained there nearly two hours, I dare say. Once I opened the yard gate and looked into the empty street. The sand, the seaweeds, and the flakes of foam were driving by, and I was obliged to call for assistance before I could shut the gate again and make it securely fast against the strong wind.

9

The part of farming enjoyed most by a boy is the making of maple sugar. It is better than blackberrying and almost as good as fishing. One reason he likes this work is that someone else does most of it. It is a sort of work in which he can appear to be very industrious, and yet do but little.

10

Rip would carry a fowling piece on his shoulder for hours together. He would trudge through the woods and swamps, up hill and down dale, to shoot a few squirrels or pigeons. He would never refuse to assist a neighbor in any way. Even the women of the village often employed him to run their little errands.

11

As far as the eye could reach the sea was of a deep blue color in every direction. The waves were running high, and were fresh and sparkling in the sunlight. In the midst lay an immense iceberg. Its cavities and valleys were thrown into deep shades. Its points and towers glittered brightly in the sun.

12

The sun pierced into my large windows. It was the opening of October, and the sky was of a dazzling blue. I looked out of my window and down the street. The white houses of the long, straight streets were almost painful to the eyes. The clear atmosphere allowed full play to the sun's brightness.

13

The success of Greeley's paper was immediate and great. It grew a little faster than the machinery for producing it could be provided. The success of the paper was due to the fact that the editor's original idea was carried out. He aimed to produce a paper which was morally helpful to the public.

14

It was one of those wonderful evenings such as are found only in this magnificent region. The sun had sunk behind the mountains, but it was still light. The twilight glow embraced a third of the sky, and against its brilliancy stood the dull white masses of the mountains in evident contrast.

15

The crown and glory of a useful life is character. It is the noblest possession of man, constituting a rank in itself, an estate in the general good-will, dignifying every station, and exalting every position in society. It exercises a greater power than wealth, and is a valuable means of securing honor.

16

George Washington was in every sense of the word a wise, good, and great man. But his temper was naturally irritable and high-toned. Through reflection and resolution he had obtained a firm and habitual ascendancy over it. If, however, it broke loose its bonds, he was most tremendous in his wrath.

17

He was six feet tall, and his body was well-proportioned. His complexion inclined to the florid; his eyes were blue and remarkably far apart. A profusion of hair covered the forehead. He was scrupulously neat in his appearance, and, although he habitually left his tent at an early hour, he was well dressed.

18

Responding to the impulse of habit, Josephus spoke and the others listened attentively, but in grim and contemptuous silence. He spoke for a long time, continuously, persistently, and ingratiatingly. Finally exhausted through lack of nourishment, be hesitated. As always happens in that contingency, he was lost.

19

The hypotheses concerning physical phenomena formulated by the early philosophers proved to be inconsistent and, in general, not universally applicable. Before relatively accurate principles could be established, physicists, mathematicians, and statisticians had to combine forces and work arduously.

20

"Read the following sentences correctly: Sophistry is fallacious reasoning. They resuscitated him. Verbiage is wordiness. Equanimity is evenness of mind. He has a pertinacious, obstinate disposition. There was subtlety and poignancy in his remarks. A hypocritical and pharisaical nature is usually cynical."

PARAGRAPH	SIXTH GRADE, STANDARD I		
	No.	Percentage	P.E.
1.....................	216	100.0	....
2.....................	216	100.0	....
3.....................	213	98.6	—3.26
4.....................	214	99.1	—3.51
5.....................	212	98.1	—3.08
6.....................	207	95.8	—2.56
7.....................	212	98.1	—3.08
8.....................	207	95.8	—2.56
9.....................	201	93.1	—2.20
10....................	199	92.1	—2.09
11....................	199	92.1	—2.09
12....................	196	90.7	—1.96
13....................	188	87.0	—1.67
14....................	186	86.1	—1.61
15....................	167	77.3	—1.11
16....................	152	70.4	— .79
17....................	163	75.5	—1.02
18....................	126	58.3	— .31
19....................	38	17.6	+1.38
20....................	6	2.8	+2.83
No. of cases......	216		

TABLE XII

PERCENTAGES CORRECT AND P.E. EQUIVALENTS FOR EACH PARAGRAPH

Paragraph	Sixth Grade, Standard I			Sixth Grade, Standard II			Sixth Grade, Standard III			Sixth Grade, Standard IV			Sixth Grade, All Standards			All Grades, All Standards		
	No.	Percentage	P.E.	No.	Percentage	P.E.	No.	Percentage	P.E.	No.	Percentage	P.E.	No.	Percentage	P.E.	No.	Percentage	P.E.
1	216	100.0	....	214	99.1	-3.45	205	94.9	-2.42	176	81.5	-1.32	811	93.9	-2.20	2,044	90.4	-1.94
2	216	100.0	....	212	98.1	-3.08	203	94.0	-2.30	172	79.6	-1.23	803	92.9	-2.18	1,914	84.7	-1.52
3	213	98.6	-3.26	206	95.4	-2.50	187	86.6	-1.64	139	64.4	.55	745	86.2	-1.62	1,764	78.1	-1.15
4	214	99.1	-3.51	208	96.3	-2.65	185	85.6	-1.58	155	71.8	.85	762	88.2	-1.76	1,728	76.5	-1.02
5	212	93.8	-3.08	200	92.6	-2.14	185	85.6	-1.58	132	61.1	.42	729	84.4	-1.50	1,573	66.9	.65
6	207	95.8	-2.56	189	87.5	-1.71	167	77.3	-1.11	131	60.6	.40	693	80.2	-1.26	1,448	64.1	.53
7	212	98.1	-3.08	185	85.6	-1.58	150	69.4	.75	101	46.8	.12	678	78.5	-1.17	1,347	50.6	.36
8	207	95.8	-2.56	190	88.0	-1.74	167	77.3	-1.11	147	68.0	.70	701	81.1	-1.31	1,333	59.9	.36
9	201	93.1	-2.20	188	87.0	-1.67	161	74.5	.98	127	58.8	.33	677	78.4	-1.17	1,300	55.8	.22
10	199	92.1	-2.09	178	82.4	-1.38	150	69.4	.75	112	51.9	.07	630	74.0	-.95	1,108	53.0	.11
11	199	92.1	-2.09	183	84.7	-1.52	106	66.9	-1.09	122	56.5	.24	670	77.5	-1.12	1,211	53.6	.13
12	190	90.7	-1.96	174	80.6	-1.28	151	69.9	.78	112	51.9	.07	635	73.5	.93	1,139	59.8	.08
13	188	87.0	-1.67	174	80.6	-1.28	145	67.1	.65	120	55.6	.21	617	71.4	.84	1,077	47.8	.09
14	186	86.1	-1.61	154	71.3	-.83	128	59.3	.35	83	38.4	.44	551	63.8	.53	945	41.8	.35
15	167	70.4	-1.11	130	59.7	-.36	98	45.4	.17	57	26.4	.94	451	52.2	.08	733	32.4	.68
16	151	70.4	-.70	107	49.5	.02	75	34.7	.58	35	16.2	-1.40	366	42.7	.57	590	26.1	.95
17	163	73.5	-1.02	119	55.1	-.10	70	32.4	.68	17	7.9	.96	366	42.7	.57	505	25.0	.50
18	126	58.3	-.31	68	31.5	+2.32	23	10.6	+1.85	7	3.2	+2.75	224	25.9	.96	330	14.6	.56
19	38	17.6	+1.38	8	3.7	+2.65	4	1.9	+3.08	1	.5	+3.82	51	5.9	+2.32	80	3.5	+2.09
20	6	2.8	+1.83	0	0.0	0.0	0	0.0	0.0	1	0.0	0.0	6	0.7	+3.65	13	.6	+3.72
No. of cases	216			216			216			216			864			2,260		

59

The Gray test paragraphs were ultimately widely used, but the benefits that could have come from them were removed later by the useless and muddying additions of tests for so-called "reading comprehension" and "fluency". Yet the original 1916 scoring on accuracy, even with its largely meaningless bow to "speed," had produced written achievement norms that were truly valid, and which could be valid and useful even today. Those crystal-clear norms had been based on the actual accuracy in reading aloud of large numbers of actual children in actual classrooms. That method of ranking, instead of averaging scores, was apparently later discarded, to judge from a later edition of Gray's test seen by this writer. Furthermore, the test was diluted by the added scoring for so-called reading comprehension, and so-called "fluency".

So far as this writer knows, no other test of simple accuracy in reading connected text, with ranked scores, has ever appeared since Gray ruined his original test and its crystal clear norms by revisions some fairly short time after its final appearance in Gray's 1916 doctoral thesis.

Apparently, only two other well-known oral reading accuracy tests were ever in use in America. (England had oral tests from their "expert," Schonell, on which I have no data.). One of those two important American tests was the Gilmore Oral Reading Test of 1951, published by Harcourt, Brace, & World, Inc., in 1951, and the Revised Gilmore Oral Reading Test of 1968. The Gilmore tests, even with their obvious defect of having been based on Thorndike's high frequency words, could have presented illuminating data on thousands of second-grade American students in 1968. That is because they were used in the United States Office of Education (USOE) 1968 testing program which compared large numbers of phonically-trained students to large numbers of students taught by other methods. (The USOE first-grade oral reading accuracy tests in 1987 had been done too early in first-grades to produce meaningful scores.)

About 1980, when this author placed a telephone call to Dr. Robert Dykstra (a strong "phonics" advocate who had worked on compiling the 1968 USOE statistics) to ask where the 1968 oral reading accuracy data for all the second-grade groups could be found, Dr. Dykstra said that someone had accidentally erased from the computer all of the 1968 statistically treated second-grade oral reading accuracy data. That data could have provided a reliable comparison between "sight-word-taught" classes and "phonically-taught" classes. That had been the only reliable large-scale study of its kind ever done in America. Furthermore, no such large-scale study was ever done after 1968, until the NAEP tests in 1992 and 2002..

The second, widely known accuracy test after those of 1916 and of 1968 was the National Assessment of Educational Progress (NAEP) testing program, carried out originally in 1992, and, with some changes in procedures, in 2002. The 1992 NAEP tests on oral reading "fluency" were the first such oral tests NAEP had ever done. However, it is not possible to consider their results as meaningful concerning the oral reading accuracy of fourth grade students. The group taking the oral test, a sub-group of those taking the 1992 NAEP written comprehension test, had been pre-screened first to judge the quality of their oral reading. If the screener felt a student had too much difficulty reading aloud the trial test, that student had been removed from the testing group. So, all real oral reading failures, or near failures, were not included, and only "successful" readers were included. No numbers were given in the official report on the Internet concerning the size of that initially rejected group.

After the screening, those remaining students were asked to re-read a selection which had already been included, with comprehension questions, on the NAEP silent reading comprehension test they had taken. That became for them a second silent reading of the same material, after which they were given reading comprehension questions to answer on the material. Then, they were asked to read the selection again a THIRD TIME, but aloud to the official scoring them. With the failing students having been removed from the so-called "test" group, NAEP concluded that the selection had been read at a 94% accuracy rate by the weaker of those finally tested orally, and at 96% or 97% accuracy by the strongest of those finally tested orally. It can only be guessed what the results might have been if the failing students had been included in those three readings, or if the students had been given a brand-new, never-before-read selection, instead of the same selection for a third time.

The 2002 NAEP test on oral reading did not focus so strongly on "fluency" as the 1992 NAEP test. It was more elaborate in its set-up. However, it also included the pre-testing and removal of students who were weak, and it included the re-reading of a selection which they had already read on the silent reading comprehension written test. It also included reading comprehension questions, like the 1992 test, but the students heard them read aloud, by the use of earphones. If the students had not been able to pronounce some of the lower frequency words when reading the selection silently, that oral recording of questions might have been very helpful, since it might have pronounced words for them that they had not been able to read previously. That might well have accounted for the 2002 increase in word accuracy scores.

What is most distressing is that the sample used for testing had already been read silently by the students at least twice, and possibly as much as three or more times before the final, at least, third re-reading. This heavy re-reading of the content comes very close to the experiences of the children whom a Welsh school inspector described, back in the 19th century. The inspector said the children had practiced their reading selections so much that they would have been able to go on "reading" if their books fell on the floor.

The claimed scores for those remaining in the test group were as follows:

Reading at 98% accuracy or above - 35% of the students tested

Reading at 95% accuracy or above - 40% of the students tested
Reading at 90% accuracy or above - 19% of the students tested
Reading below 90% accuracy - 6% of the students

The tests described above were all of connected text, as in Gray's reading paragraphs. However, the only other, well-known tests of oral reading accuracy are not on connected texts, but on lists of increasingly difficult words.

The first such well- known test was about 1923, written by Arthur Irving Gates of Columbia Teachers College. Like William Scott Gray, Gates had been a graduate student at Columbia Teachers College under Thorndike, was teaching there with Thorndike in 1923, and became the author of the other deaf-mute-method reading series published in the early 1930's, the Macmillan, in 1931.

The second well-known test of reading lists of progressively more difficult words is the Slosson Oral Reading Test (1990 and later by Richard Slosson and Charles Nicholson).

The third is the Samuel L. Blumenfeld listing of such words (The Blumenfeld Oral Reading Assessment Test, 2015 and 2018, The Paradigm Company.)

Gates published the results from classes using his circa 1923 test, which could provide a norm for anyone wishing to duplicate his work. Revisions of Gates' material is probably still sold for individual use in reading remediation, but obviously the norming would be different. Slosson probably provided adequate norms for reading his lists of words since he did show purported grade levels for achievement. Whether Blumenfeld's test had norms is also unknown. However, the Slosson word lists are available since his text is reportedly still in print, and, so far as is known, is still in use. It could provide some reliable data on accuracy in reading lists of words of increasing difficulty.

However, considering the blatant inadequacies of the NAEP statistics on oral reading accuracy on connected texts, those NAEP statistics cannot be accepted as a norm for 4th grade oral reading accuracy when reading connected texts. Neither can the later versions of Gray's oral reading test be used to determine the oral reading accuracy of American students as the test has been altered. In all probability, since the Gilmore test was composed by Gilmore's deliberate use of words under the 10,000 frequency level as listed in Thorndike's work, neither can the Gilmore norms be used to judge reading accuracy levels when the material has an uncontrolled, natural vocabulary, such as in the Bible.

Therefore, the record shows a woeful lack of any kind of well-known reliable grade-level statistics concerning oral reading accuracy in reading connected texts, other than Gray's Standard 1 1916 results.

APPENDIX A-1

To Provide Some Usable Test Data and Information Concerning Oral Reading Accuracy

To provide concrete oral-reading-accuracy statistics at a second-grade level, following is a summary of material from this writer's half-year 1977-1978 sabbatical in this country and Europe. At that time, she observed the teaching of reading in first grades, and then tested the oral reading at second grades in the same schools.

In 1977 and 1978, America had two dominant methods in use, the vastly greater sight-word use, and the far smaller "phonic" use. In Europe, the sight-word "global" programs were far more sound-oriented than the American sight-word programs. For rating the teaching of reading in first grades as observed by the writer, she used a scale of 1 to 10. A score of 1 meant the heavy use of sight-words, and 10 the heavy use of phonics, with mixtures falling in between. None of the European schools observed by this writer rated a score lower than 6. (Current reports are that such a happy condition no longer exists, particularly in France.) Yet, the American sight-word classes observed by this writer rated scores of 2 or 3, and only one rated a score of 5. American sound-oriented classes rated scores of 7 to 10.

In all, about 900 second graders in this country and Europe were tested with a 144-word selection, the first five of the forty items in Booklet 3J, Reading Speed Test, copyrighted in 1969 by IEA (International Association for the Evaluation of Educational Achievement, Stockholm, Sweden). Permission was granted by IEA to use this short five-item selection, with the understanding that IEA would be acknowledged in any written material resulting from the research.

It was the simple vocabulary of the first five items which made it appropriate for a second-grade test. The 144-word total contains 64 different words, and 40 of them are on the 250 commonest words in English (the Ladybird Key Words Reading Scheme). Most of the rest are on the Thorndike list of the 500 most common (The Teacher's Word Book of 30,000 Words, Thorndike and Lorge, 1944). Only 11 of the 64 words are above the 500 most common. Of the 11, 6 are on the list from 500 to 1,000 (brown, catch, dog, gray, leg, spot), and 5 are above the 1,000 frequency (Peter, trick, fed, hind, puppy). When a child missed a word, he was told it, and so should have been able to read it the next time he saw it.

It was necessary to have the short selection translated by a commercial translating company into Icelandic, German, Dutch, French and Swedish, for use as needed. The high-frequency effect applied for other languages.

The writer requested permission from the education authorities in some New Jersey municipalities, and in Iceland, Luxembourg, Belgium, Holland, Sweden, Germany and France, to observe teaching of reading in first grades, and then to test oral reading in second grades at those same schools. Because of the remarkable and much appreciated courtesy from these authorities in granting this permission and arranging school appointments, it became possible to carry out the oral reading research in the fall and winter of 1977-1978.

It should be emphasized that the selection of children was made by chance, sometimes a whole class if time permitted, and sometimes those closest to the window or door. None of the selections of children were made ahead of time, and no prior contact had been made with any of the teachers of the classes. The test-giver and the teachers met for the first time at the classroom doors.

The 144-word selection was almost completely of high-frequency words, because it is impossible to test sight-word trained children on anything with a normal vocabulary. For instance, it would not have been possible to use a selection from <u>The Child's Garden of Verses</u> by Robert Louis Stevenson, because it has a normal vocabulary. However, that book had been appropriate for second grades until the deaf-mute-method readers arrived after 1930.

Therefore, the passing scores in sight-word-trained classes might have been failures if the children had been asked to read a whole poem from Stevenson's book or to read anything else with natural vocabulary. A Houghton-Mifflin second grader tested in January, 1978, scored at 99% accuracy on this 144-word test of mainly very high-frequency words. She was wearing a sweatshirt with a large word printed over and over on it. When asked what the word was, she said it was "Australia." The word was not "Australia. It was "outrageous." Yet she had scored at 99% on this oral-reading-accuracy test. Even though she scored at 99% accuracy in reading, the truth is that the little girl was really illiterate, in the real meaning of the word "illiterate" - being unable to deal with letters.

Concerning failures, for the American sight-word classes in January, one-quarter, or 25% failed, scoring below 90% accuracy. For the January "phonic" classes, only 8% failed, which meant that 92% had passed.

At the higher level of accuracy, for the January American sight-word classes, 53% scored at 95% accuracy or higher, which was approximately half of the classes. However, for the American "phonic" classes, 77% scored at 95% accuracy or higher, and that was more than three-quarters of the classes.

The full statistics for all classes are published in the writer's book, <u>Why Jacques, Johann and Jan CAN Read</u>.

Some of the test results which were obtained for individual classes will be shown below.

Even though the "meaning" method for teaching beginning reading had been promoted widely since the early 19th century, a more elaborate approach arrived at the beginning of the 20th century, and it was the product of the early psychologists.

As has been previously mentioned, William James, who was the first American psychologist, wrote a paper in 1904, <u>Does Consciousness Exist?</u> In it, he said:

"The word consciousness is just a loose way of indicating that certain sensory occurrences form part of my life history."

Obviously, some time before James wrote this 1904 paper, he effectively denied the existence of consciousness.

For a 1908 book, <u>Essays Philosophical and Psychological in Honor of William James</u>, Thorndike wrote a chapter, "A Pragmatic Substitute for Free Will." In it, he reportedly discussed free will by such things as instinctive responses and the resultant habits developing from them. It therefore appears that, some time before 1908, Thorndike had also thrown consciousness, and its free will, into the discard, just as James had done by 1904.

It might be assumed that the materialistic convictions of James and Thorndike were shared by many of their influential academic associates and co-workers after 1908, and influenced their work as well, just as it had influenced James and Thorndike. It was on that hard-rock, materialistic and atheistic basis that the oxymoron, "reading comprehension" was born and promoted by these people. Yet, so far as can be determined, no one had ever heard of a "skill" called "reading comprehension" until the advent of William James and his associates such as Thorndike. Even the idea that such a skill could exist was brand new on the face of the earth. Apparently, that idea grew out of the denial of consciousness and free will.

"Listening" is automatic. Our brains automatically turn a stream of sound into a stream of language, which automatic product is then presented to our conscious minds to understand. Reading should just be a form of listening, and therefore produce the same kind of automatic language stream that can be presented to our conscious minds to understand. As discussed earlier, the act of reading (turning print into language) properly done, is an automatic skill, emanating from a part of the brain that stores skills but lacks consciousness. However, understanding that decoded language ("comprehension") can only take place in a part of the brain that is conscious.

If the conscious mind does have to be involved in the decoding of the language stream, it is a disability. People have no problem conceding that fact when the decoding concerns spoken language. Hard-of-hearing people consciously guess the blurred parts of language they cannot hear, and that is uniformly regarded as a disability. Reading disabled people do the same thing concerning the blurred parts of print they cannot "hear" but that is regarded, not as a disability, but as the use of the famous reading method, "psycholinguistic guessing."

However, Thorndike and James did not believe in the existence of consciousness and the conscious mind, and they lived long before the neurosurgeon Dr. Wilder Penfield identified the automatic and the conscious areas of the brain through his decades of surgery on the brains of living people.

For James and Thorndike and their followers in their post-1908 world, every action had to be automatic, and had to grow out of previous automatic actions, and that meant "reading comprehension" had to be automatic. "Choosing" was a term that could only mean to them that a new series of stimulus-response associations was being put into action, triggered by an automatic response that was labeled a "choice." Therefore, for them, there could be no such thing as a freely-chosen conscious choice in anything, such as "choosing" or "not choosing" to pay attention when reading. Reading, and attention when reading, like every other action, had to be purely automatic, simply the result of a long line of previous stimulus-response associations.

As his 1890 text showed, James had been fascinated by the soundless reading of deaf-mutes who had not been taught to speak, but only to use sign language and to read by meaning-bearing sight words. Even though teaching the deaf to speak very well had been done successfully for over a hundred years in America and Europe, speech was not taught in most American schools for the deaf at that time, such as the Gallaudet school. Instead of learning to speak (and to lip read) normal speech, the Gallaudet approach was to teach silent sign language and to teach reading by meaning-bearing sight-words. Yet there was a movement in America in the 1860's to teach the deaf to speak, and to found such a school for the deaf. Some years previously, Alexander Graham Bell's deaf wife spoke normally and had learned lip-reading.

James should have been very familiar with the two opposite approaches since there had been a very public conflict and discussion of the two methods in Boston in the late 1860's. In 1869, Superintendent Philbrick founded a day-school for deaf children, who were taught speech and lip-reading. That was about the time that James was a medical student at Harvard, across the Charles River from Boston. Even Alexander Graham Bell, the famous inventor of the telephone, had some involvement. For many years, his father, Alexander Mellville Bell, had worked on teaching the deaf to speak, and to read normally. In the well-known movie, My Fair Lady, Professor Higgins, the speech expert, is shown working with Bell's charts. Bell's charts did, indeed, exist, and had been invented by Alexander Melville Bell, to teach the deaf to speak.

However, with the Gallaudet-style soundless deaf-mute, sight-word method, the getting of some "meaning" from a text was guaranteed. It was a simple, mechanical, stimulus-response, two-step connection from perceived print to perceived meaning, and James should surely have understood that. When reading isolated words, there could be no intermediate, possibly stumbling step, from print to sound and only then to meaning.

As has been discussed, teaching hearing children in American schools to read by that pure deaf-mute method began in 1930 with the readers written by James's "academic grand-children", William Scott Gray and Arthur Irving Gates. Both men had been graduate students of William James's student, E. L. Thorndike. Gray and Gates brought into America's unfortunate schools the vast, workbook-paper-wasting and years-long teaching of that non-existent, "skill," so-called "reading comprehension." Huge mountains of workbook pages have been filled in by America's children ever since 1930, writing their silent answers to the workbooks' silent "reading comprehension" questions, so that they would become accomplished "psycholinguistic guessers". Not only were forests of trees wasted making the paper in those workbooks, but so were huge amounts of schoolroom time wasted that should have instead been spent in learning history, geography, mathematics, grammar, and real literature.

Even sound-based beginning reading programs in America waste vast quantities of time teaching so-called "reading comprehension." Yet in Europe, before 1977, even though the "global" method (sight-words) was sometimes heavily promoted, there was apparently no great emphasis on teaching "reading comprehension." Therefore, any influence from the heavy teaching of so-called "reading comprehension" should be absent from test results from European schools, and the results should more clearly show the natural differences between the methods.

Following are two graphs showing the results that were obtained when the same "reading comprehension test" was given to two separate groups of children in Europe in October and November, 1977. The teaching observed in first grades had been rated on a scale from pure "meaning" or sight words at Code 1, and pure "sound" or so-called phonics at Code 10, with relative mixtures falling in between. The European classes, because of the heavier phonic emphasis in first grades, were graded no lower than Code 6, but as high as Code 10. After those observations had been done in first grades, second grades in the same schools were tested.

One graph is made from the 101 individual "comprehension" scores of children in the 1977 European second-grade Code 6 schools, where more emphasis on "meaning" in first grades had been observed. The other graph is made up from the 237 individual "comprehension" scores of children in the 1977 European second-grade Code 7 to Code 10 schools, averaging about Code 9, where children had been taught with far less "meaning" emphasis in first grades. Except for that difference in teaching methods, the background of each group seemed to be very much the same. They appeared to be normal grade-school populations in each country.

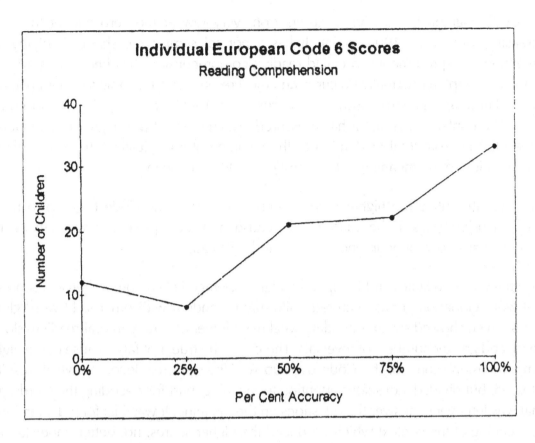

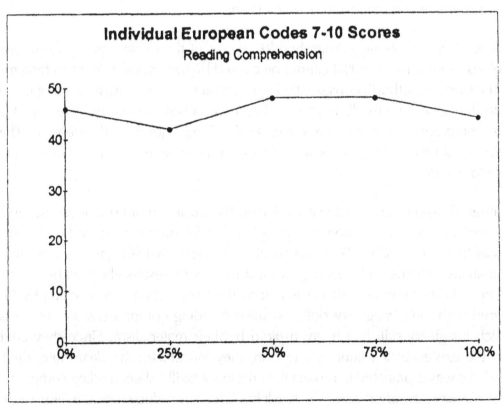

The Code 6 graph has a normal curve, from very low at the zero end of the scale, increasing toward the 100% point. It has a normal semi-curve shape, implying that something real (presumably so-called reading comprehension) has been measured. Yet the Code 9 graph has virtually no curve and most resembles a flat table top. It is an almost straight line reaching across from zero accuracy to 100% accuracy. That is no normal curve. The contention is that it has measured nothing except the degree of attention of the test-takers, from total inattention to the meaning of the questions (0% accuracy) to total attention to the meaning of the questions (100% accuracy.)

However, attributing the higher comprehension scores of the Code 6 group to higher comprehension "skills" is the fallacy of false cause (non causa pro causa) when that which is not the cause of a phenomenon is taken to be its cause.

In both the United States and Europe, the higher averaged class comprehension scores of sight-word/global programs occurred uniformly in tandem with other sight-word/global scores which showed severe decoding weakness: lower accuracy in oral reading, slower speed, and greater numbers of reversals. Therefore, the true, not false, cause of the higher comprehension scores of the Code 6 group was their poorer decoding which resulted in forced, but divided, conscious attention to meaning, part for decoding the words, and what was left over to answer the questions on the meaning. It was that forced attention to the meaning of the context which produced the higher scores, not better understanding of the meaning in comparison to phonic classes.

The huge spread in phonic comprehension scores of the Code 9 group from terrible to marvelous (from zero to 100%) cannot be caused by the phonic initial teaching method, since the Code 9 method's consistently high accuracy scores show no kind of correlation at all to the Code 9 method's totally random comprehension scores. Those widespread phonic comprehension scores were the result of free, not forced, attention. That free attention could either freely choose to focus on the meaning of the selection or freely choose to wander.

The James/Thorndike et al materialists denied the existence of consciousness, and, with it, the existence of free attention. Their explanation for such widespread comprehension scores as those of the Code 9 classes would have been that such scores were the result of an inability to focus on "meaning." It must have been results like the above on which the James/Thorndike et al materialists placed their conviction that teaching by "sound" interfered with their imaginary skill, so-called "reading comprehension," the existence of which imaginary skill had been inspired by their materialism. Since they could not accept the existence of voluntary attention, they introduced the deaf-mute, right-brain method that was guaranteed to protect the imaginary "skill," silent reading comprehension. Instead, for over a hundred years, the result has been to produce untold millions of reading disabilities.

The following tables concern some of the research data reported in <u>Why Jacques, Johann and Jan CAN Read</u>, (1979, 2004, 2008) by Geraldine E. Rodgers. One concerns the total research, but the others concern only a few of the schools in New Jersey, U.S.A.; Luxembourg City, Luxembourg; Stockholm, Sweden; Hamburg, Germany; Innsbruck, Austria, and Avignon, France.

The first table, "On the Consistent Profile of Arrows...." demonstrates the difference in results in this oral reading study from teaching by "sound" or teaching by "meaning." When higher codes are compared to lower codes, a consistent pattern of scores (arrows) appears. Higher codes score higher in word accuracy, and speed. Lower codes score higher on reversals and on that non-existent so-called skill, reading comprehension, the meaninglessness of which has been discussed. The higher score reveals a forced, but divided, attention. Part of the attention is spent decoding the words. Only what is left over can be spent understanding the text.

However, the near-perfect consistency in the arrows' directions when comparing higher codes to lower codes shows the presence of a force in action, which force is presumed to be a conflict between conditioned reflexes.

It should be noted that two classes were omitted from this study because they had not been fully tested. Since adequate time had not been available for enough students in those two classes to take the test, each student read only part of the test. Those incomplete class scores have been omitted. Also, scores are omitted from any second-grade students who had not been in the same school in first grade.

The next tables report on two schools in the United States, one a Code 10 school and the other a Code 2 school. Those two schools can be compared for differences in results between teaching beginning reading by the "sound" of print or by the sight-word "meaning" of the print.

Following that are tables reporting on schools in Luxembourg, Sweden, Hamburg, Innsbruck and Avignon, with Codes shown for each school. Those tables are self-explanatory.

———————— ✦✦✦✦✦✦ ————————

On the Consistent Profile of Arrows When Comparing Phonics Scores to Sight-Word Scores -

Totals for the second-grade level on oral accuracy reading tests given to 495 American children in English and 338 European children in German, Dutch, Swedish, and French.

On the 1-to-10 Code scale, 1 is total sight-word teaching and 10 total phonic teaching, with mixtures ranging from Code 2 to Code 9 Compared to Code 9. Ratings were based on observations in first grades in schools where second grades were tested. The near-perfect consistency in the arrows' directions on this table of oral reading research results, when comparing higher codes to lower codes, shows the presence of a force. It is concluded that the force is the conflict between mutually exclusive conditioned reflexes for processing print, (or between mixtures of these reflexes).

	Per Cent Passing Accuracy		Per Cent Passing Comprehension	Estimated Speed		Per Cent Reversals
	At or above 95% on Test	At or above 90% on Test		% Slow	% Fast	
U. S. Fall 1977 Phonic Code 9.4 Compared to U. S. Sight-Word Code 2 Sept. to Mid-Oct	58>37	78>42	58<63	15<26	10>0	9<16
Europe Fall 1977 Phonic Code 8.6 Compared to Europe Sight-Word Code 6 Mid-Oct to End of Nov.	90>74	96>86.5	44<57	17<37	26>10	6<18.5
U. S. January 1978 Phonic Code 10 Compared to U. S. Sight-Word Code 2.9	77>53	92>75	*51<68	8<15	35>14	6<11
U. S. January 1978 Phonic Code 10 Compared to Europe Fall 1977 Sight-Word Code 6	77>74	92>86.5	*51<57	8<37	35>10	6<18.5
Europe Fall 1977 Phonic Code 8.6 Compared to U. S. January 1978 Sight-Word Code 2.9	90>53	96>75	44<68	**17>15	26>14	6<11
U. S. Jan. 1978 Code 3 Houghton Mifflin Compared to Code 2 Scott Foresman	55>42	74<68	62<68	16<17	8<13	11<13

Oral Accuracy Per Cent	Number of Pupils Obtaining Score	
100	3	
99	4	
98	1	
97	1	Pupils Scoring
96	2	95 or Better
95	2	13 of 16 or 81%
		Pupils Scoring
		90 or Better
94	1	14 of 16 or 88%
89*	1	
80*	1	

Comprehension of Five Questions

Per Cent Correct	Number of Pupils Obtaining Score	
		Pupils Scoring
100	5	80 or Better
80	4	4 of 16 or 56%
60	4	
40	2	
Incomplete Fail	1	

Rate: 2 of 16 slow, or 13%
7 of 16 fast, or 44% fast.

Reversals: 1 of 16, or 6%

Notes: The child with the score of 89 had severe reversals and was being referred for psychological testing because of difficulty not only with reading but with math. The child with the score of 80 is hearing disabled.

This teacher said she believes in phonics and stresses it. She permits quiet talk in the classroom.

Individual Scores in Order Tested

Accuracy/Comprehension

99-60   Fast

99-60   Fast

80-60   Slow. Hearing problem. Scheduled to have operation. Reversals, 3 times: spot~stop

96-40

100-80   Fast

98-100   Fast

94-100   Slow

99-100

95-60   Slow

97-80   Good rate

96-80   Fast

89-Incomplete. Very slow with severe reversals Being referred for testing. Also has trouble with math.

100-100   Fast

99-100   Good rate

95-40   Fair rate

100-80   Fast

U. S. 26 - Code 2 - Scott, Foresman - 17 Pupils Present, All Tested, January, 1978

Oral Accuracy Per Cent	Number of Pupils Obtaining Score	
100	1	Pupils Scoring
99	4	95 or Better
96	3	8 of 17 or 47%
		Pupils Scoring
		90 or Better
93	4	12 or 17 or 71%
88	2	
86	1	Below 85 - None
85	2	

Comprehension of Five Questions

Per Cent Correct	Number of Pupils Obtaining Score	Pupils Scoring
100	5	80 or Better
80	8	13 of 17 or 77%
60	2	
40	1	
20	1	

Rate: 4 of 17 slow, or 24%
2 of 17 fast, or 12%.

Reversals: 1 of 17, or 6%.

Two pupils absent.

Retentions: In this school last year, one of three or four first grade teachers held 2 back.
Whether other first-grade teachers did is unknown.

U. S. 26 - Code 2 - Scott, Foresman - 17 Pupils Present, All Tested - January, 1978

Individual Scores in Order Tested

Accuracy/Comprehension

99-80

96-100

93-80   Fairly slow

99-80   Fast

96-100

100-80 Points with finger, constantly losing her place.

99-80   Good rate

96-100 Fast

85-80   Substitution, non-phonic: many~middle

86-60   Slow

99-60   Black (In contrast to this Code 2 program, NO
European Black student tested, who were all
from Code 6 or higher programs, failed
comprehension.)

88-80   Very non-phonic substitution: learned~listened

93-20   Fairly slow

88-40   Slow. Very non-phonic substitution:
second~shoulder.

85-100 Fair rate. Very non-phonic substitutions:
small~shell, learned~lemon.

93-80   Slow, reversal: number~under.

93-100 Slow

<u>Luxembourg - Code 8, Text: Toni, Bim, Lee, Karin, Ann -
Tested 12 of 18 Pupils Present, October, 1977</u>

Oral Accuracy <u>Per Cent</u>	Number of Pupils <u>Obtaining Score</u>	
100	3	
99	3	
98	3	Pupils Scoring
97	1	<u>95 or Better</u>
96	1	<u>11 of 12 or 92%</u>
		Pupils Scoring
91	1	<u>90 or Better</u>
		12 of 12 or 100%

<u>Comprehension of Last Four Questions</u>

Per Cent <u>Correct</u>	Number of Pupils <u>Obtaining Score</u>	Pupils Scoring
100	1	<u>75 or Better</u>
75	2	<u>3 of 10 or 30%</u>
50	4	
25	3	
Incomplete	2 (One too slow, one insufficient time)	

Rate: 4 of 12 slow, or 33% slow.
       1 of 12 fairly fast, or 8% fairly fast.
       None fast.

Reversals: 1 of 12, or 8% reversals.

This was a school with many foreign children in a poorer residential area. The children were chosen by me in the order in which they were seated, by rows. The teacher said those whom time did not permit to test were neither brighter nor duller than the rest. Perhaps one-third repeated first grade because of the language problem. Luxembourgers speak German and French. In restaurants and elsewhere, they switch back and forth from French to German many times in a conversation. Most of these students spoke a different language at home, but were taught to read in German in first grade. Then, in second grade, instruction was in French. That these largely foreign second-grade children could read at all seems miraculous, but that none failed accuracy is even more astonishing. However, their slow speed in reading German in second grade is certainly understandable.

Individual Scores in Order Tested

Accuracy/Comprehension

99-100
96-75   Slow
97-25   Slow
100-50
99-50
100-75 Fairly fast
98-66   Incomplete, only through item 3, because too slow.
98-50
91-25   Slow
98-50   Reversal: Fleck~felck.
99-25
100-Incomplete through item 1, no time.

Stockholm 2 - Code 8, Text: Nu Laser and Language Experience
Tested All 15 in Class, November, 1977

Oral Accuracy Per Cent	Number of Pupils Obtaining Score	
100	6	
99	1	
98	3	
97	1	Pupils Scoring
96	1	95 or Better
95	1	13 of 15 or 87%
94	1	Pupils Scoring
91	1	90 or Better
		15 or 15 or 100%

Comprehension of Last Four Questions

Per Cent Correct	Number of Pupils Obtaining Score	
100	7	Pupils Scoring
75	5	75 or Better
		12 of 15 or 80%
50	1	
25	2	

Rate: 4 of 15 slow, or 27% slow.
       3 of 15 fast, or 20% fast..

Reversals: 4 of 15, or 20% reversals.

Retentions: None mentioned.

Individual Scores in Order Tested

Accuracy/Comprehension

99-50
96-25   Slow
100-100⁻
98-100 A little slow
100-75 Fast
100-75 Fast
91-100 Reverses syllables, boll~blau
100-100
94-100 Very slow. Reversals: 5 on b-d.
98-100 Faster
95-75   Slow. Two reversals: kallar~klaller,
        berattelsen~berattlesen (pronounced "lee").
97-25   Slow. Omitted "st" in "konster." For "bakbenen,"
        read "bakstassen." For "konsten," read
        "bonsten."
100-75
98-75
100-100

Hamburg 2 - Code 10. Text: Bunte Welt - 14 of 16 Children Present Tested. November, 1977

Oral Accuracy Per Cent	Number of Pupils Obtaining Score	
100	3	
99	1	
98	6*	Pupils Scoring
97	1	95 or Better
96	2	13 or 14 or 93%
		Pupils Scoring
91	1	90 or Better
		14 of 14 or 100%

*One incomplete. Read 2/5 because of lack of time.

Comprehension of Last Four Questions

Per Cent Correct	Number of Pupils Obtaining Score	
		Pupils Scoring
100	6*	75 or Better
75	1	7 of 14 or 50%
50	2	
25	2	
0	3	

One incomplete. Read 2/5 because of lack of time.

Notes: 14 of 16 children in this afternoon half of the class were chosen by chance selection. All these children read at a good rate - no dragging except on occasional long words. This was a poor residential neighborhood.

Rate: None slow.
   4 of 14 fast, or 29% fast.

Reversals: 1 of 14, or 7% reversals.

Retentions: None mentioned..

Individual Scores in Order Tested

Accuracy/Comprehension

*100-75 Fast

*97-100 Fast

*98-50 Fast

*98-0

*91-0 Added "en" to many words, to the amusement of the Rector and myself. Without these, the score would be 98%.

*96-100

100-0

99-50

98-25

98-100 Appeared to be Indian or Pakistani. Reversals: bekam~dekam, twice.

100-25 Fast. Appeared to be foreign.

98-100

96-100

98-100 Read only 2/5. No time.

*Woman Rector observed as these first children were tested.

Innsbruck - Code 10, Text: Kommt, Wir Wollen Lesen und Schreiben - 28 in Class, All Tested, November, 1977

Oral Accuracy Per Cent	Number of Pupils Obtaining Score	
100	2	
99	4	
98	6	
97	5	Pupils Scoring
96	7*	95 or Better
95	2	26 of 28 or 93%
		Pupils Scoring
93	2	90 or Better
		28 of 28 or 100%

*Two of the seven took only part of the test because time ran out.

Comprehension of Last Four Questions

Per Cent Correct	Number of Pupils Obtaining Score	
		Pupils Scoring
100	4	75 or Better
75	7	11 of 26 or 42%
50	7	
25	7	
0	1	
Incomplete	2 (not enough time)	

This class dismissed at 11:00 a. m. this day, so there was no time to complete testing on all children, despite the remarkably rapid rate at which they read: 13 of 28, or 46%, read either fast, very fast, or very, very fast. Only one read slowly (4%) but tested at 96% accuracy. The teacher considered this to be an average income neighborhood.

Rate: 1 of 28 slow, or 4%.
        13 of 28 fast, or 46% fast.

Reversals: 1 of 28, or 4% reversals.

Retentions: None mentioned..

Individual Scores in Order Tested

Accuracy/Comprehension

100-50 Fast
97-25 Fairly fast
93-25 Average
93-100 Very fast
96-50 Good rate
97-25 Fast
100-25 Good rate
95-75 Reversal: Fleck~felck
97-100 Good rate.
98-75 Good rate
97-50 Fast
96-25 Good rate
95-75 Good rate
99-100 Fast
98-75 Fast
98-50 Fast
96-50 Very fast
99-75 Fast
96-50 Fast
96-25 Slow
99-100 Very fast
98-75 Very fast
98-50 Very, very fast
98-75
99-25 Satisfactory
97-0 (First 3 questions only)
96-Incomplete (One question - no time)
96-Incomplete (One question - no time

Oral Accuracy Per Cent	Number of Pupils Obtaining Score	
100	8	
99	6	
98	4	Pupils Scoring
97	4	95 or Better
95	1	23 of 27 or 85%
		Pupils Scoring
		90 or Better
93	1	25 of 27 or 93%
91	1	
80	1	
70	1	

Comprehension of Last Four Questions

Per Cent Correct	Number of Pupils Obtaining Score	
		Pupils Scoring
100	2	75 or Better
75	6	8 of 27 or 30%
50	5	
25	6.	
0	8 (One incomplete)	

Rate: 3 of 27 slow, or 11% slow
7 of 27 fast, or 26% fast

Reversals: 1 of 27 or 4%

The teacher considered that the children who scored 70 and 80 "could only read a word here and there." She said she would send me the slow ones first.

Retentions: One mentioned, the girl who scored 80, who had repeated two years.

Avignon 4 - Code 9. Text: Experience Charts Teaching Heavy Phonics,
With Syllable Emphasis - 27 Children in Class, All Tested - November, 1977

Individual Scores in Order Tested

Accuracy/Comprehension

93-0   Very slow
80-25   Slow. Girl, retained twice.
91-25
95-0   Good rate.
97-25   Good rate
98-50   Fair rate
97-25   Fair rate
97-25   Fair rate
70-Incomplete. Read 61 words. Boy. Read very, very
          slowly. Reversal: d'annees~de-na.
100-100 Fast
98-75   Good rate
99-75
100-50   Common French Errors
100-75   Fast   Observed in Most Programs
98-50
100-25   Fast   chemin~chien
97-0   Good rate   reçu~reku
100-75   Fast   balle~table (a few)
98-0
99-50   Fast   Most make liaisons
100-75   Fast   correctly. Almost never do they
99-0   Fair rate   read silent consonants. One
99-100   Good rate   did, who read perfectly
100-0   Fast   otherwise but said the "t" in
99-0   Good rate   "est" and "c'est."
99-50   Good rate
100-75

In the "slow ones" that this Avignon teacher sent me first, none passed comprehension or
read fast. Yet 7 of the 9 (78%) passed the accuracy test, scoring above the "frustration"
level at 90 or higher. Also, 5 of the 9 (55%) read at the "instructional level" of 95 or
higher. This teacher really knew her second-grade class, as every one one of the
remaining 18 not only read above the frustration level (at 90 or above) but read at the
"instructional level" of 95 or above. Also, 7 of the remaining 18 read fast (or 39% of the
18), and 8 of the remaining 18 (or 44%) passed comprehension.

Her "slow" second-grade group in November, with 7 of the 9 (78%) scoring above frustration (90 or above) and 5 of 9 (55%) scoring at the "instructional level" of 95 or above, was almost identical but slightly higher than U. S. sight-word classes two months later in January (75% above the "frustrational" level and 53% at the "instructional" level). This is despite the fact that this teacher's "slow" group included two of the three worst readers I tested in France, and two of the six worst readers I tested in Europe (excluding a brain-damaged child and two children who had not learned the language in which I tested them.) If these two highly unrepresentative children are omitted from this Avignon teacher's scores, then 100% of the remaining 7 children in her second-grade "slow" group scored above the frustration level (at 90 or above) and 59% of her "slow" group scored at the "instructional" level (95 or above). That would make her second-grade "slow" group in November superior to ALL of the U. S. second-grade Scott, Foresman and Houghton Mifflin sight-word classes that I tested about two months later, in January.

The testing in American and European schools, as reported here. was done by a single American teacher, who had no official help or official financial backing of any kind whatsoever, except for the kind cooperation of officials in the places tested. With the vast sums of money spent on education in America, there is therefore absolutely no reason why such simple testing cannot be carried out and recorded in schools all over America.

In 1992 and 2002, NAEP removed weaker readers from their test groups and then gave printed material to the rest of the groups, which material each student had read at least two times silently, and as slowly as desired, before finally being asked to read it a third time orally. Such a program was incapable of producing meaningful results on oral reading accuracy.

Yet it should be very easy to find what the real facts are about actual oral reading accuracy of all American students, not just for a pre-selected and pre-practiced group as in the essentially meaningless NAEP oral reading accuracy research. The United States really does not need any such costly, influence-affected, agency as the NAEP to do that job. In towns all over America, as this private 1977-1978 research has demonstrated, people can do it for themselves.

APPENDIX B

Concerning the Carefully Buried 1915 Ayres Spelling Scale
With Its Shocking Proof of Almost Universal Literacy in 1915 American Children,
At Which Time They Were Taught to Read by Supplementary Phonics ("Sound")
(A Revision of Chapter 29 from The Hidden Story, 1998, by this Writer)

In 1920, the famous and highly influential psychologist, Edward L. Thorndike, of Columbia Teachers College, wrote an article which appeared in Harper's Magazine, entitled "The Psychology of the Half-Educated Man." In that article, Thorndike said we should depend on "experts" to do our thinking for us in all areas except those that concern our everyday work. Thorndike wrote:

"In his special field, the size and character of which will vary with his talents, a man may be made a competent thinker.... Outside that field, the intelligent procedure for most of us is to refuse to think, spending our energy rather in finding the expert in the case and learning from him.... Wherever there is the expert.... should we not let him be our guide? Should we not, in fact, let him do our thinking for us in that field?"

Yet, as this history demonstrates, it is exceedingly hurtful to become the obedient serfs of "experts." Of course, as this history also demonstrates, Thorndike was himself one of the very worst of the "experts," whose advice he said the public should mindlessly follow.

Such "experts" in education as Thorndike chose to bury inconvenient truths about which their obedient serfs were supposed to remain ignorant. Two of those inconvenient truths appeared in Leonard P. Ayres' A Measuring Scale for Ability in Spelling, published in 1915 by the Russell Sage Foundation, New York, and republished in 1986 by Mott Media, Milford, Michigan, but with different page numbers, and an appendix. (It also had a foreword wrongly attributed to me which had been an attempt to summarize one of my papers, but it was in different words and with factual errors.)

Ayres' sources for his word list had been The London Point System of Reading for the Blind, by Rev. J. Knowles in England in 1904, Six Thousand Common English Words, by R. C. Eldridge of Niagara Falls in 1911, Ayres' own study, The Spelling Vocabularies of

Personal and Business Letters in 1913, and The Child and His Spelling, by W. A. Cook and M. V. O'Shea in 1914.

The first inconvenient truth contained in the Ayres scale was the extremely high achievement on written spelling tests on the 1,000 commonest English words, which tests Ayres gave to 70,000 children at mid-term in grades 2 to 8 in 84 American cities in 1914 and 1915. Ayres' high scores demonstrated that America had no spelling (and therefore virtually no reading) problem in 1914 and 1915 when supplemental phonics ("sound") was used in beginning reading.

Ayres' 1914-1915 scores contrast most appallingly to the spelling scores reported on The New Iowa Spelling Scale of 1954, and presumably on any elementary-school scales after about 1940. By 1940, the vast majority of American elementary-school children had been taught to read by the deaf-mute-method ("meaning") readers. They used the phony "intrinsic" phonics that had been introduced in 1930 and 1931 by Thorndike's ex-students, Arthur Irving Gates and William Scott Gray, instead of the formerly widely used supplemental phonics (true "sound"). Therefore, by 1940, the disastrous results from the deaf-mute method would show up on spelling tests.

The Iowa-scale spelling scores in the 1950's demonstrated, beyond any possible doubt, the resultant, absolutely enormous, drop in spelling achievement since the Ayres' statistics of 1915. Yet it is almost beyond comprehension that such an historically-demonstrable and statistically-demonstrable enormous drop has gone TOTALLY UNPUBLICIZED! However, by the 1950's, public awareness of the 1915 once-famous Ayres scale - and the scale itself, had been effectively buried.

The enormous, almost unbelievable, drop can be demonstrated by comparing spelling scores on specific words obtained by Ayres at mid-term of second grade in 1914 and 1915 to scores on those same words obtained by the Iowa-scale tests in the early 1950's at beginning second grade. The Iowa-scale test results for beginning second grades were published in The New Iowa Spelling Scale, State University of Iowa, Iowa City, Iowa, 1954. Like the Ayres scores, the Iowa-scale scores were based on huge numbers of tests, given to 30,000 children in the early 1950's. Ayres had tested 70,000 children in 1914 and 1915.

However, the enormous differences between the Iowa-scale 1950's scores and the Ayres 1915 scores cannot be explained away just by the half-year difference in testing, from beginning second grade (Iowa-scale scores) to mid-second grade (Ayres scores). In case anyone doubts that fact, he can look up the beginning-third-grade Iowa-scale scores in the 1950's, which are almost as bad as the beginning-second-grade scores, and far worse than the mid-second-grade Ayres' 1915 scores.

The Ayres scale from A to Z for spelling scores on the 1,000 commonest English words had been arranged in increasing order of difficulty, from the easiest A list to the hardest Z list. The Ayres A and B easiest lists contained only six very easy words (A: me, do; B: and, go, at, on). However, the approximate first half of the Ayres scale, including Levels A and B through Level L, totaled 447 words. All Levels, A through Z contained all of the 1,000 commonest words.

Below are scores on some words, taken from the second-grade 1954 Iowa scale, matched to the scores for those same words on the 1915 second-grade Ayres scale from C to L in difficulty.

Ayres' scores for individual words are not statistical abstractions, except for some small rounding out, as if scores of 5, 6, and 7 were all reported as 6. Except for such "rounding out," Ayres individual scores were based on concrete test results which showed how many children could or could not spell a particular word. Therefore, the data on individual words is NOT an average, but a factual report on the per cent of successes and the per cent of failures for children on that particular word. That is why the figures at the head of each column apply equally to every single word in that column. The figures report the percentage of children who did or did not spell those individual words correctly in 1914 and 1915. That concrete data on scores reported by Ayres is very arresting, since it can be compared to the exact same kind of concrete data on the Iowa-scale 1950's scores.

Ayres did not bother to report any word scores below 50% accuracy. Ayres stated (on page 37 of the 1915 Russell Sage edition, and on page 23 of the 1986 Mott Media edition):

"All of the scales have been arbitrarily cut off at 50 per cent, partly because it is doubtful whether any useful teaching purpose is served by testing children on words of which they cannot spell more than 50 per cent correctly...."

Yet the scores for the vast majority of the 1950's second-grade scale words, 52 of the 61 words which were also on the Ayres scale, were below the 50% score that Ayres considered should be a reasonable cut-off point!

Those 52 words appeared on the Ayres scale up to List L, but his second-grade scores for those words in 1914-1915 ranged from 98% correct to 50% correct, in comparison to Iowa-scale's range for those same words from 49% to 3%. Only 9 Iowa-scale words out of the 61 (see, can, run, the, up, like, come, had, play) scored at 50% or above. They probably received massive practice in the deaf-mute-method readers after 1930, such as "see" (98% Iowa pass) as in "See, Spot," and the unphonetic word, "come," (79% Iowa-scale pass) as in "Come, Spot." Yet a totally phonetic word, "bring," somewhat related in meaning to the unphonetic word, "come," had only a 9 per cent Iowa-scale pass, in contrast to the 79% Ayres pass on "bring"!

Therefore, in 1915, only 21% of mid-second graders failed to spell the completely phonetic word, "bring," correctly, but, in the early 1950's, 91% of beginning second graders failed to spell that completely phonetic word! The problem did not lie in the half-term difference, since Iowa-scale beginning third-grade scores were almost as bad as the beginning second-grade scores. After viewing the spelling scores, it is impossible to doubt that a massive change must have taken place by the 1950's in the way children perceived word structure. That change, of course, is explained by the move after 1930 from teaching beginning reading by "sound" to teaching beginning reading by "meaning."

It is astonishing that the 1915 Ayres scale showed that 100 per cent of seventh graders (not second graders) in 1915 could correctly spell EVERY SINGLE WORD on the Ayres lists from A to L, which is about half of the thousand commonest words in English. That kind of score, 100% spelling 100%, is NOT a statistical abstraction, except possibly for a very tiny rounding out of scores.

If the argument is made that the weakest children had dropped out of school by seventh grade, that argument can be dismissed by citing the fifth grade scores. In his 1909 study, Laggards in Our Schools, published by The Russell Sage Foundation, New York, Leonard Porter Ayres had shown that the vast majority of American city children did not repeat more than two years in school. In 1914-1915, most city children could not leave school before about the age of 14. For his spelling scale, Ayres tested only city children in 84 cities in 1914 and 1915, and only 7 of those cities were in the South where truancy laws were not so effective. Therefore, because almost no American city children were more than two years behind in school for their age, and since most American city children could not leave school before age 14, that means Ayres' scores at fifth grade represented most American city children, including "left-backs," the weakest students.

Ayres showed that, at fifth grade, 100% correctly spelled all the words through list H, for a total of 137 words out of the thousand commonest, and 99% correctly spelled all the words through list I for a total of 200 words out of the thousand commonest. Such children could obviously read a great many more words than they could spell correctly. Therefore, Ayres' scores obviously indicated virtually 100 per cent literacy in American city school children in 1915 (and therefore probably in most other American children, since truancy laws were widely enforced).

Of the 1,000 words on the Ayres list, only 61 were on the Iowa list. Below is a comparison of the scores for 30 of those 61 words, at five of the Ayres-scale accuracy levels:

1915 Ayres 1954 Iowa

like	88	52
of	88	38
him	88	41
out	88	46
come	84	79
had	84	50
play	84	61
let	84	28
are	84	34
say	84	30
for	79	47
led	79	11
get	79	42
some	79	38
has	79	28
stand	79	8
bring	79	9
that	79	30
how	79	38
was	79	49
eat	79	41
first	58	8
they	58	39
sent	58	5
could	58	3
where	58	12
fell	50	12
stop	50	39
wish	50	5
right	50	4

The Ayres' tests were dictated, written spelling tests. The Iowa-scale tests most likely were on the multiple-choice forms which had been promoted about 1930 by "experts" as superior for testing. Yet written tests like Ayres' 1915 tests require "recall" memory, while multiple choice tests which were probably used in the l950's require only "recognition" memory. That is obviously a far lower and far less useful form of learning.

The 1954 second-grade Iowa scale, when contrasted to the 1915 second-grade Ayres scale, clearly established that there had been a huge drop since 1915. Besides the second-grade comparison given above, it would also be of great interest to prepare lists for the third through eighth grade levels so as to show 1915 Ayres scores in contrast to 1950's Iowa-scale scores for those words which appeared on both scales at each grade level. I know from a casual review of 1950's Iowa-scale scores at the third grade level that they were also exceedingly low.

Burdette Ross Buckingham had received his doctorate from Columbia Teachers College in 1913 for his thesis, Spelling Ability, Its Measurement and Distribution. His 1913 work was very much overshadowed by Ayres' 1915 A Measuring Scale for Ability in Spelling, published by the Russell Sage Foundation in New York.

In July of 1918, the College of Education at the University of Illinois, at Urbana, Illinois, established the Bureau of Educational Research, and Buckingham was appointed its director. In November of 1919, he published a report on its first year's work, which had been extensive. Buckingham wrote, on page 9 of his report (available on the Internet):

"The Bureau publishes far the greater part of the test materials it distributes…. The Bureau is the sole distributor of the following tests…."

In the list that followed, Buckingham included Buckingham's Extension of the Ayres Spelling Scale, so it was apparently solely published by the University of Illinois and in print some time after July, 1918, when the Bureau opened. It is unknown if the scale had already been in print by others in some form before 1918, but it was also published by others some time after November, 1919, when Buckingham wrote his report. After about 1919, the Buckingham version appears to have been heavily used in the United States. It seems to have displaced the far superior 1915 Ayres scale in the 1920's. Buckingham's material must have been heavily promoted by the education "experts", largely from Columbia Teachers' College and the University of Chicago.

Buckingham's version added 505 words to Ayres' 1ist, claiming those 505 words were common in spelling books. (That was, of course, an extraordinarily unintelligent reason for extending Ayres' carefully crafted scale of the commonest words,)

Ayres' scores had been mid-term scores, half-way through the year. Yet Buckingham, on his "extension" of Ayres' scale, misquoted Ayres by falsely stating that Ayres' mid-year scores had been end-year scores. Of course, children can learn more in a half year, so the use of Buckingham's version obviously lowered expectations.

Buckingham then misquoted others of Ayres' statistics, which misrepresentations sharply lowered spelling norms. Ayres had printed his lists of words, from A to Z, in columns. Over each column, Ayres had shown the score achieved for that column at each grade level. For instance, over the list of 52 words in Column H, Ayres showed that the 1915 second-grade scores were 79% accuracy, third-grade scores were 92% accuracy, fourth-grade scores were 98% accuracy, and fifth-grade scores were 100% accuracy. Ayres listed nothing for grades six, seven and eight, because those upper grades also had 100% accuracy on the 52 H words.

Concerning the interpretation of such percentages which were shown at the top of each column of words, Ayres had stated (on pages 36 and 37 of the Russell Sage 1915 edition, and on page 22 of the Mott Media 1986 edition):

"The limits for the groups are as follows: 50 means from 46 through 54 per cent; 58 means from 55 through 62 per cent; 66 means from 63 through 69 per cent; 73 means from 70 through 76 per cent; 79 means from 77 through 81 per cent; 84 means from 82 through 86 per cent; 88 means from 87 through 90 per cent; 92 means from 91 through 93 per cent; 94 means 94 and 95 per cent; 96 means 96 and 97 per cent; while 98, 99 and 100 per cent are separate groups."

So, for each reported percentage point, Ayres had included only a few scores below and a few scores above to complete a point's range (as for 66, three points below and three above).

Therefore, the only percentages actually appearing on Ayres' scale were 50, 58, 66, 73, 79, 84, 88, 92, 94, 96, 98, 99 and 100, so scores falling in between those numbers had to be defined in terms of those percentages, which Ayres did very clearly, as shown in the above quotation. As discussed, he did not bother to report any scores below 50%. Yet he explained (on pages 30 and 31 of the 1915 edition and on page 19 of the Mott 1986 edition), that he originally had:

"...a total of 25 steps for the entire scale from 0 to 100.... These 25 values are 100, 99, 98, 96, 94, 92, 88, 84, 79, 73, 66, 58, 50, 42, 34, 27, 21, 16, 12, 8, 6, 4, 2, 1, 0. They have been used to identify the 25 steps and they indicate the average per cent of correct spellings found among the children of the grade in question.... For example, the nine words, the, in, so, no, now, man, ten, bed, top, are shown on the scale as at step 94 for the second grade. This indicates that the average per cent correct among second grade attempts to spell these words was 94."

Yet Buckingham deliberately distorted those carefully-spelled-out, and very narrow, ranges in his "extension" of the Ayres scale, which distortion greatly dropped expectations. Furthermore, Buckingham showed scores below 50%, even though Ayres' had never reported those scores, either in his book or on his paper scale accompanying his book. Where did Buckingham get those less-than-50% scores for Ayres' tests, since Ayres specifically stated he was not including them? Yet, without any explanation, Buckingham sometimes showed those low scores for Ayres' scale just as if they had originally appeared on Ayres' published scale. Were those below-50%-accuracy scores for Ayres' data pure fabrications by Buckingham, like Buckingham's report on the ranges of Ayres' percentages?

Buckingham's report on the ranges for Ayres' percentages is shown below. Buckingham's huge and wide ranges for each percentage point are, indeed, the purest of fabrications, just like Buckingham's statement that Ayres' percentages represented achievement at the end of the school year, when Ayres had specifically stated they were mid-term scores.

Printed below are the grade level percentage scores that Buckingham gave for the scale's word at Column O, (27%, 50%, 73%, 84%, 92%, 96%, 99% and 100%.) Except for inserting an imaginary 27%, they are the same as Ayres, but what he does with the ranges to use for each score is appalling and very different from Ayres. Therefore, for comparison, inserted after each of Buckingham's percentage ranges for Column O, are the very different percentage ranges, far higher and smaller, that Ayres had given for those same points on his scale..

Buckingham wrote:

"Since the per cents given in each column are for the end of the school year, [In error: Ayres had said mid-term] the per cents are the upper limits for the given grades. Thus, for Column O, the complete ranges of per cents are as follows:

"27 means from 12 through 27 and equals second grade ability; (Not included at all by Ayres)
50 means from 28 through 50 and equals third grade ability; (Ayres range: 46 through 54)
73 means from 51 through 73 and equals fourth grade ability; (Ayres range: 70 through 76)
84 means from 74 through 84 and equals fifth grade ability; (Ayres range: 83 through 86)
92 means from 85 through 92 and equals sixth grade abilty; (Ayres range:91 through 93)
96 means from 93 through 96 and equals seventh grade ability; (Ayres range: 96 and 97)
99 means from 97 through 99 and equals eighth grade ability; (Ayres gave only 99)
100 equals ninth grade ability." (Ayres did not show 100 under Column O and never listed ninth grade ability anywhere.)

Ayres had reported narrow ranges both above and below each averaged percentage point. Yet Buckingham reported NOTHING ABOVE for his "averaged" percentage points (gutting the whole idea of "an average").

Buckingham's statistical ranges were given only BELOW each point and were as wide as 23 at a point under O, 24 at a point under Q, and as wide at other points. Yet Ayres largest range below any point was only 4, not 24! Most of Ayres' "below" ranges were not 4, but 3, 2, or 1.

Since Ayres' predominant skill had been his remarkably adept handling of statistics, I wonder what Ayres might have thought of Buckingham's irrational and apparently imaginary "statistics" for a scale that Ayres himself had invented?

Even as early as 1918, Ayres' high scores must have been very embarrassing to the group promoting "meaning" instead of "sound" in the teaching of beginning reading, men like Edward L. Thorndike's associate, Arthur Irving Gates at Columbia Teachers College, and like Charles Hubbard Judd's associate, William Scott Gray at the University of Chicago. The scores coming in from the very extensive city testing of the pre-1920 period must have revealed the great drop in spelling achievement if children were taught by sight-word "meaning" instead of phonic "sound." Since Buckingham's circa 1918 scale greatly dropped expectations for spelling achievement by partially gutting the Ayres scale, it must have been, temporarily, a great consolation. Yet it also was buried from sight shortly after 1930, because the scores coming from the new deaf-mute-method classes could not even begin to meet Buckingham's lower standards.

It is curious that Buckingham's once-famous version of the Ayres scale is not even listed in the Columbia Teachers College Library card catalog, as I learned when I called there in 1995 to get the exact date of the publication of Buckingham's scale materials (which scale materials I later found elsewhere). I assumed it had been published about 1919 at Columbia Teachers College, where Buckingham received his doctorate on spelling work in 1913, but my photocopies of Buckingham's "extension" do not include the title page with the date and the publisher. What is quite certain from those photocopies, however, in comparison to Ayres' material, is that Buckingham deliberately altered Ayres' statistical data, and that Buckingham's deliberate alterations resulted in lowered expectations for spelling achievement. That, of course, raises serious questions about Buckingham's motives for altering those statistics.

However, the Ayres scale in its original 1915 version, particularly in relation to the 1950's Iowa scales, clearly established that America had no spelling (and therefore virtually no reading) problem in 1915. The existence of the 1915 Ayres spelling scale by 1930 (and even the less threatening 1919 Buckingham extension of that scale) were obviously potential sources of enormous embarrassment to the "experts" who were promoting the deaf-mute-method meaning readers in 1930.

For those "reading experts, a second inconvenient reality had been demonstrated by the Ayres scale, even worse than the statistical demonstration that American children could spell - and therefore read - very well in 1915.

Ayres' 1914-1915 work on spelling scores had been done with his previously unpublished but statistically-arrived-at list of the thousand commonest words in English. Ayres' list of the 1,000 commonest words (something never reported before) had been based two-thirds on personal and business letters, and one-third on literature and newspapers. Thorndike had also been working since 1911 to identify the commonest words, but he did not publish his book on the 10,000 commonest words until 1921.

In his 1915 book, Ayres showed each word in its precise statistical order of frequency. By grouping Ayres' words and adding each word's statistics, it had become possible to show that only a thousand of the commonest words are used to cover more than 90% of almost anything in print. It was that newly-demonstrated fact about word frequencies, about how few words it takes to say so much of any page, which was so very inconvenient for the 1930 deaf-mute-method texts. That is because it was that otherwise hidden fact which had made it possible to teach beginning reading to hearing children without the use of any sound at all, as if the children were totally deaf.

As reported in my 1995 history, the high-frequency-word concept did previously appear on pages 22 and 23 of Joshua Leavitt's Primer: or Little Lessons for Little Learners, Leavitt's Reading Series,

Part I, published by John P. Jewett & Co., Boston, 1851, and copyrighted in 1847. The probability is that the high-frequency-word concept had first arrived in America with Thomas Hopkins Gallaudet, when he returned from studying in the deaf-mute school in Paris. Leavitt listed eleven words presumed to form one-quarter of anything we read, and a further list of 68 words which, with the first eleven given, were presumed to form half of any written material. Leavitt's 1847 list of 79 words forming one-half of written material includes many words on Leonard P. Ayres' 1915 list of the 50 words which Ayres found to compose half of written correspondence, as discussed in his A Measuring Scale for Ability in Spelling, pages 7 through 12 (and 1 through 5 of the Mott edition). It is interesting that the nine words which Ayres found to comprise one-fourth of all written material are ALL on Leavitt's list of the eleven words forming one quarter of all texts. Leavitt also included "it" and "is" in his list of those words comprising one-quarter of any text. However, Ayres lists "it" as the eleventh commonest word, and "is" as the thirteenth.

The probability is that Leavitt's 1847 list was originally based, not on scientific word-counts like the lists Ayres used, but on texts such as Gallaudet's that were used for deaf-mutes. Of course, that greatly reduced the size of the deaf-mutes' ultimate vocabularies, in comparison to the vocabularies of people who could "hear" new words (whether spoken or written) or of deaf persons who have been taught speech and who have been taught to read by phonics. The latter can therefore add the words they "hear" through reading to their ultimate vocabularies.

However, any longer lists of high-frequency words for deaf-mutes than Leavitt listed, which might have been prepared before Ayres began his work, could not have been very reliable. If reliable lists of high-frequency words for the teaching of deaf-mutes had been in existence, Ayres certainly would have referred to them and used them, since he did refer to and use three other scientific studies that had been done besides his own.

The only other published acknowledgment I have found from before about 1986 of the high-frequency effect came from England. A brochure was published in 1969, <u>The Ladybird Key Words Reading Scheme, Notes for Teachers.</u> The following appears on page 3:

"The scientific basis of the reading scheme is the use of 'Key Words'* This is the name given to a group of the most used words of the language. Recent research has established that a relatively few English words form a very large proportion of those in daily use. The diagram printed below indicates this.."

The asterisked footnote read, "Key Words to Literacy, by J. McNally and W. Murray, published by the Schoolmaster Publishing Co., Ltd., London….." It then read, "A review comment on this research '…it is a promising step forward in our progress towards universal literacy….' (Educational Psychologist, Teachers' World, May 25, 1962),"

That comment, "…it was a step forward," concerning the "Key Words" research" certainly indicates that the 1962 reviewer had never heard of the once-famous 1915 Ayres material. It seems fairly certain that neither had the researchers.

The diagram was a square, divided into sections, and was meant to represent the relative use of different words in a presumed average total adult vocabulary of 20,000 words. The first quarter of the square, meaning one-quarter of an adult's speech, contained only 12 words. That obviously meant that those 12 words comprised one-quarter of anything the adult said. The next quarter of the square contained two entries. A smaller entry at the top, in larger print, contained 20 words. The rest of the square, in smaller print, contained 68 words. A note next to those top two quarters of the square read, "the total… shows that 100 words make up 1/2 of those in common use." A line was drawn slightly below the rim of the bottom half, with the words, "a further 150", with an extra 50 words not shown. The total of 300 words were the words on which the Ladybird series was based.

Shown on the cover of the booklet was the following: "W. Murray, the author of the Ladybird Key Words Reading scheme, is an experienced headmaster, author and lecturer on the teaching of reading. He is co-author, with J. McNally, of 'Key Words to Literacy,' a teacher's book published by "The Schoolmaster Publishing Co., Ltd., Derbyshire House, St. Chad's Street, London, W.C.1."

In a series of little reading books, the Ladybird series taught those 300 highest frequency words, a few at a time, in an organized sequence. They are charming little books, very worth having in a primary classroom's library for children's individual use, as I know from having had them in my personal classroom library when I was teaching. They should also be very useful in teaching English to non-English-speaking children. However, if used to teach beginning reading, they certainly would result in teaching children to read by "meaning" and not by "sound," and would produce the same kind of problems as the deaf-mute readers.

Nevertheless, W. Murray and J. McNally, who are apparently the ones who produced the study on the frequency of words on which the Ladybird series is based, deserve great praise. They are the only people, to my knowledge, who did essentially what Ayres did on word frequency statistics, but Ayres had the whole resources of The Russell Sage Foundation to fund his work. Yet there is no indication whatsoever that Murray and McNally had ever heard of Ayres' 1915 work, because their work had been called, in 1962, "recent research." The 1962 review of their work cited above called it "...a promising step forward." The review obviously meant that it was a new step.

Many lists of highly used words have been published since Ayres' day, but, so far as I know, none give the information on the precise portion of texts occupied by these words, as Ayres and the Ladybird publishers did.. One such massively used word list which apprently lacks that totaled information is the "Dolch" list, and there are others. So far as I know, they all lacked the critical information from the Ayres' scale, which is to show how much of a text's space is occupied by their word list.

However, as discussed, Ayres' scientific listing of the thousand commonest words in the precise statistical order of their descending frequency had clearly shown that the one thousand highest-frequency words compose over ninety per cent of most texts. It was precisely that astonishing fact which made it possible to use the deaf-mute, context-guessing method on hearing children, and not just in first grade, but all through their schooling and throughout their entire lives. That is because the ability to read at least ninety percent of a text is presumed to make it possible to guess the meaning of the rest of any text. Such readers can be presumed to be reading above the so-called "frustration level" for the understanding of the text.

Thomas Hopkins Gallaudet founded the first successful American school for the deaf, about 1818. He became quite famous, and was also active later in promoting government schools to replace non-government schools. In 1835, Gallaudet published The Mother's Primer, meant to teach beginning reading to both hearing and deaf children. In it, he used the same method he had formerly used in his school for deaf-mutes. "New" words were only introduced in texts containing about 90% of previously taught words. That 90% level presumably provided sufficient context on which to guess the meaning of a new word, and, of course, the "meaningful" guess had nothing to do with sound. Children were learning to read words only by their meaning, and with no dependance at all on sound.

In his 1973 book, The New Illiterates, Samuel L. Blumenfeld cited Gallaudet's The Mother's Primer as the probable source and model for the 1930 and 1931 deaf-mute-method reading series produced by William Scott Gray and Arthur Irving Gates, Thorndike's former graduate students.

Like The Mother's Primer, both series used contexts of memorized words to aid in guessing unknown words. Samuel Blumenfeld could not find a copy of The Mother's Primer in any library, despite many efforts. I finally located and received a photocopy from the Gallaudet College library.

The idea of using a 90% accuracy score for reading words in a text as a "passing" score for understanding a text most probably was based on that 1835 book of Gallaudet's, which he had published for both deaf and hearing children. It is also interesting that a score of about 93% accuracy, close to 90%, was considered a passing score for the reading of William Scott Gray's 1917 oral reading paragraphs. That suggests that Gray may have been familiar with Gallaudet's method before 1914 when he began to assemble those paragraphs. Also, when I was taking graduate courses on "reading instruction" about 1971, a score of 90% accuracy in reading texts orally was considered a "passing" score for being able to understand a selection's meaning. The influence of Gallaudet's Mother's Primer seems obvious.

Although Ayres did not use my term, the "cumulative high-frequency-word effect," the concept was nevertheless clearly explained by Ayres in 1915, and he provided the most crystal-clear supporting statistics to support the fact that only 50 words are used in producing half of almost any text, and only about 1,000 words are used in producing 90% of most texts.. Yet the cumulative high-frequency-word effect was very carefully hidden by Edward L. Thorndike in the 1944 third version of one of his works, which version was written with Irving Lorge, The Teacher's Word Book of 30,000 Words, Teachers College Press, Teachers College, Columbia University, New York. It had very possibly also been hidden in Thorndike's second version of that work in 1932, which had a total of 20,000 words.

The first version was written only by Thorndike in 1921, carrying the title, <u>The Teachers'</u> <u>Word Book</u>, and it contained the 10,000 commonest words. Yet the high-frequency-word effect was not so completely masked in the original work, because Thorndike did at least group the 100 commonest words and the 200 commonest words, and perhaps more groups, in the original edition. However, he did not say what portion of most texts would be occupied by the 100 commonest, or 200 commonest, etc. Except for the low frequency words, Thorndike did not give the words' individual ranking, at Ayres had done. In the 1944 edition, Thorndike listed only the 500 commonest and 1,000 commonest but gave no supporting statistics. However, it is interesting that, in the 1944 edition, for words above the 2,000 most common, he did give each word a ranking as Ayres had done for all of the 1,000 commonest.

Ayres showed the number of occurrences for each word in 100,000 running words of average texts. The 50 most frequent words had 49,615 occurrences in those 100,000 words. It becomes self-evident that only 50 words can comprise one-half of average material. Ayres found that only 1,000 words comprised almost 92% of his 100,000 running words.

Whether Thorndike gave ranking statistics for each word in his two editions before 1944, as Ayres had done, is unknown, as those volumes are not available to this writer. Without those supporting statistics, the high-frequency-word effect is hidden.

The fact that E. L. Thorndike did originally at least list in 1921 the one-hundred and two-hundred commonest words (but probably not their supporting statistics) turned up in a 1923 book. The book had been published by The Macmillan Company and was entitled, <u>Everyday Classics, Teachers' Manual</u>, by Fannie Wyche Dunn, who was an assistant professor at Columbia Teachers College. (E. L. Thorndike's brother, Ashley H. Thorndike, Professor of English at Columbia, was one of the authors on <u>Everyday Classics</u>.) Dunn wrote the following on page 4, showing in a footnote, "Thorndike, E. L., <u>The Teachers'</u> <u>Word Book</u>."

"Just as we have for several years had a list of the thousand most commonly written words as an aide to our emphasis in teaching spelling, we now have a list of the ten thousand most commonly printed words to aid us in our emphasis in the teaching of reading. This list, moreover, shows the first hundred words in reading importance, the second hundred, the first five hundred, the first thousand, and so on…."

Even though Thorndike hid the cumulative high-frequency-word effect in his own published work in 1944 (and probably in his two earlier editions of that text), he had to have known about it from his own initial, personal, massive word counts of the 10,000 commonest words, which he had carried out from about 1911 to 1920. Of course, Thorndike also had to know about it from Ayres' well-publicized 1915 study of the thousand commonest words, in which the exact frequency for each word was also shown.

Ayres wrote in 1915 (pages 10 and 11, and page 4 of the Mott edition):

".....These [1,000 commonest] words, together with the figures showing the frequency of appearance of each, per 100,000 running words, are given in List A beginning on page 12. The figures inserted after each 50 words show the cumulative frequencies from the beginning. Thus the first of these figures shows that the 50 commonest words are repeated so frequently that with their repetitions they constitute nearly half of all the words we write. The first 300 words make up more than three-fourths of all writing of this kind and the 1,000 words with their repetitions constitute more than nine-tenths of this sort of written material."

The earlier studies that Ayres cited could have revealed the facts concerning the 50 and perhaps even the 300 commonest words, if it had occurred to anyone to add the total occurrences together (for every 50 words) as Ayres did, with his "cumulative frequencies." However, those earlier studies were obscure, scholarly things, which would have to be searched out on library shelves by people who, for some reason, had their interest aroused in those studies. As far as the public was concerned, those studies had effectively been buried, already, long before 1930. Yet Ayres' material was something very different. Ayres book (Part 1) contained the background on his scale, and the separate paper scale itself (Part 2) had obviously been printed separately for ease of use in classrooms. The paper scale was also sold separately, originally only for five cents. Both parts had obviously been published for ordinary school administrators and ordinary school teachers, in ordinary schools, all over America, the very same market that the 1930 deaf-mute-method readers were to invade. Therefore, unlike those earlier vocabulary studies that mentioned word frequencies, the Ayres' spelling material was not something that automatically buried itself in large and ignored libraries.

The probability is that Ayres spelling scale of 1915 had once been massively used, since it is certain that his handwriting scale of 1917 was massively used. Victor H. Noll discussed Ayres' handwriting scale on page 180 of Introduction to Educational Measurement, published by Houghton Mifflin Company, Boston, in 1957. Just before his material on Ayres, Noll had discussed the (Edward L.) Thorndike Scale for Hand-Writing of Children, Teachers College, Columbia University, 1910. Thorndike's was the first "scale" ever constructed from a large base of individual responses. The writing of 1,000 children from Grades 5 to 8 had been ranked by judges, and the resultant ranks provided the handwriting samples which were then published to demonstrate "Quality 4" to "Quality 18" in handwriting. After discussing Thorndike's handwriting scale, Noll then said:

"Another scale similar to that of Thorndike is the Ayres Scale, often referred to as the Gettysburg Edition."

In a footnote, Noll showed that it had been published as "Measuring Scale for Handwriting: Gettysburg Edition (New York: Russell Sage Foundation, 1917)."

Noll continued:

"This was one of the most widely used scales ever devised, over 600,000 copies having been printed between 1917 and 1935. It derives its name from the fact that the opening lines of Lincoln's 'Gettysburg Address' are used as the subject matter. The teacher writes on the board the first three sentences of this address and instructs his pupils to read and copy until familiar with it. They then copy it, writing with ink on lined paper for exactly two minutes. The scale includes eight samples of levels of quality, grades from 2 to 8. The pupils' writing is compared with the samples for quality, and the total number of letters written in the two minutes is counted.

"Norms are given for both speed and quality for Grades 2 to 8....."

What is astonishing is that in 1957, Victor H. Noll, a professor (and presumably psychologist) at Michigan State University, who obviously knew all about Ayres' handwriting scale, had nevertheless apparently never heard of Ayres spelling scale! That Noll had not done so is strongly suggested by the fact that Noll DID refer on page 20 to the first study of spelling accuracy ever published, that of Dr. J. M. Rice, who gave nation-wide tests of spelling in 1895 and 1896.

Rice published the completed data in <u>Scientific Management in Education </u>in 1913. The 1913 copy I saw was published by Publishers Printing Company. Noll cited "New York: Hinds, Noble and Eldredge, 1914". The material had appeared first in the New York magazine, <u>Forum,</u> in 1897.

As discussed in my 1995 history, Rice had found great fault with what he called the "spelling grind" in American schools. Astonishingly, Rice had no knowledge that the "spelling grind" had resulted by about 1889 because of the enormous failures when spelling was almost thrown out of schools after 1875 because of Colonel Parker's influence. Education memory was as astonishingly short in the 1890's as it is today. However, when Rice gave massive spelling tests in 1895 and 1896, he discovered that American students were excellent spellers by that time. Obviously, the "spelling grind" after about 1889 had worked.

The second problem arising from the Ayres scale was even worse than the first, its spelling data. The second problem was the Ayres' paragraph concerning cumulative word frequencies, and the tables reporting cumulative frequencies at the end of Ayres'

1915 book. They were sheer public-relations poison for the two proposed 1930 and 1931 deaf-mute-method reading series by Gray and Gates. That is because Ayres' figures on word frequencies could show that people could give the illusion of "reading" if they knew only the 1,000 commonest words (or even the 300 commonest) out of the half million or more words in English, if they could guess "psycholinguistically" the rest of the context. Such "psycholinguistic" drill had been built right into the 1930 deaf-mute-method reading books.

Because of the cumulative high frequency word effect, children at higher grade levels could stumble through most books and mislead even their teachers. The deaf-mute, sight-word, context-guessing method can certainly give the illusion of success. Proper tests for reading competence, such as grade-level, hand-written, spelling tests and tests for oral reading accuracy, had largely disappeared from classrooms by 1930. They had largely been replaced by the so-called "silent reading comprehension" tests, which test intelligence, not reading accuracy. By such fake "testing," the fact would be hidden that children might no longer read uncontrolled vocabulary materials by themselves. (like the Bible, for instance).

However, the "experts" testing house of cards might collapse if the "wrong" people ever got the Ayres testing material. Ayres data could reveal the astonishing fact that an illiterate who can recognize only1,000 of the highest frequency words can produce the illusion that he is not an illiterate.

In her 1967 book, Learning to Read: The Great Debate, Jean Chall confirmed the existence of the resulting reading problem from the sight-word series by 1951. On page 294, Chall quoted an unnamed curriculum supervisor:

"...a weak spot was in word perception (recognition and analysis). Since we also had complaints from the fourth-, fifth-, and sixth-grade teachers that the children could not sound out new words when they left the highly controlled vocabularies of the basal readers, we decided that a stronger phonics program was in order."

Children could score very well on the so-called "silent reading comprehension tests" at the so-called lower-grade reading levels in reading when the vocabulary was still rigidly controlled in all their textbooks. Yet children began to have great trouble with their so-called "reading comprehension" at the so-called higher-grade reading levels when books began to be used with uncontrolled, low-frequency vocabulary.

We hear today that the only real reading problems are with so-called "reading comprehension" at the high school and college levels. The "experts'" house of cards would, indeed, collapse if the public ever really understood, as they could from the cumulative high-frequency-word effect demonstrated by the Ayres scale, that the real "reading" problem has nothing to do with so-called "reading comprehension." The real reading problem is instead the simple fact that most children can comfortably read only a relatively small number of sight words out of the half million or so in English. They cannot really read, but can only guess, any words outside the small number that they have succeeded in memorizing by their appearance.

The truth is that about half or perhaps many more of Americans under seventy years of age today are unable easily to pronounce and therefore to deal with the lower frequency words, such as the words in high school and college texts, even with the "help" of ludicrous, context-guessing, "intrinsic phonics." The real reason for the so-called low "reading comprehension" of so many of our high school and college students is their very real ILLITERACY. They can really only recognize ("read") a sight-word base composed for the most part of the highest frequency words. They are not suffering from something called "functional illiteracy," because so-called "functional illiteracy" is just another fake term invented by "experts." They are, instead, really illiterate.

By 1930, the "experts" HAD to know that most students did not have any real success using context-guessing "intrinsic phonics" on brand new words in reading, particularly when their reading texts became really difficult as at the high school and college levels. The "experts" had to know that they were condemning half or more of American children to lives crippled by so-called "functional illiteracy," and that even the "successful" half after 1930 would not be able to read with the easy automaticity of earlier days.

If the Ayres scale were still in circulation after 1930, the public might find out the truth. They might then openly oppose the deaf-mute method as soon as it began to take over American schools shortly after 1930.

The 1915 Ayres scale could prove not only that a huge drop in spelling scores resulted when the deaf-mute method was used. It could reveal to the public that such a surprising thing was in existence as the cumulative high-frequency-word effect, and that it could hide true illiteracy. It is obvious that the Ayres spelling scale of 1915 posed a very real public relations problem for the change-agents at William Scott Gray's University of Chicago and Arthur Irving Gates' Columbia Teachers College, who were busy in the 1920's writing the deaf-mute-method reading series that were totally dependent on the cumulative high-frequency-word effect for their very existence.

Therefore, it is anything but surprising to learn that a great deal of successful effort went into burying the Ayres scale. What happened to the Ayres' scale is surely one of the most classic examples of Unthink in the twentieth century.

Even references to the once-famous Ayres scale apparently disappeared from the literature after about 1932, except perhaps for a brief account on the nature of the Ayres scale that I found in a 1938 book in the New York University library. The book was entitled Psychology of Elementary School Subjects, and was written by William Henry Gray, Ph. D. (not William Scott Gray), and was published by Prentice-Hall, New York. William Henry Gray was an Associate Professor of Psychology at Kansas State Teachers College of Emporia. The reference to the Ayres scale in that 1938 book, which I first saw in the spring of 1981 while browsing almost randomly through the New York University library stacks, started my search for a surviving copy of the Ayres' scale. (What I actually wrote that afternoon in 1981 in the margin of the photocopy I made of that page of that 1938 psychology book was the very unacademic word, "Wow!) If I had not seen the reference to the Ayres scale in that 1938 book, I would never have known of the nature, and probably not even of the existence, of the 1915 Ayres scale. Nor, obviously, would I have learned of its careful burial.

In May, 1981, when I first tried to locate a copy of the Ayres scale, after having learned of its existence from the 1938 book just mentioned, I called the scale's original publisher, the Russell Sage Foundation, in Manhattan. I spoke to a man who said he had begun there in 1943. He said that, although at one time they had printed Ayres' spelling scale and Ayres' handwriting scale, they no longer did so. The education department of the foundation had been disbanded in 1948, and he said a great deal of the education material was sent to Columbia University Library, and a smaller portion to the New York Public Library. I then called the New York Public Library, and they said they did have a copy. However, I did not look up that copy until a few years later, and it turned out to have been a numbered volume in a complete set of the Russell Sage Foundation publications on education, which showed no titles on their bindings, but just the volume's number in the set. That copy, with only Russell Sage Foundation No. 139 (and possibly "Recreation (and Education) Departments"), printed on its outside binding, was stamped as having arrived in the New York Public Library in 1915. No other copy was available, so obviously the New York Public Library did not get another copy from the Russell Sage Foundation in 1948.

Next, since I had been told that the bulk of the Russell Sage Foundation education material went to Columbia University in 1948, I decided it would be easiest to ask my local library to request an inter-library loan of a copy of the Ayres scale, and my local library did so. I did eventually receive what was apparently the sole copy in the Columbia Teachers College library, and it had arrived in the Columbia Teachers College library in 1934, according to the first date on the check-out sheet at its back. I received that copy under the puzzling circumstances described below.

Numerous copies of the Ayres scale, properly labeled and filed, might have been anticipated to have been in the Columbia Teachers College library since they received most of the Russell Sage Foundation education material in 1948. Nevertheless, the Columbia Teachers College library did not have a single copy from that 1948 Russell Sage Foundation source, and had only one surviving copy. That copy had arrived in 1934, but the library check-out sheet and card in its back cover clearly showed heavy erasing, on top of which was mislabeling. The book had been misfiled under that inaccurate title, and with no author shown, ever since 1934. Why was that single surviving copy mislabeled, after erasures had been made on its check-out sheet and card? Furthermore, since the great amount of material which was sent in 1948 from the Russell Sage Foundation to Columbia almost certainly included copies of the Ayres scale, what happened to them?

Except for that sole copy which only appeared in the stacks in 1934 under the wrong title and with no author shown, the once-famous Ayres scale almost totally disappeared at Thorndike's Columbia Teachers College, The pasted-in check-out sheet at the back of the book, which had been erased and relabeled, showed the first date of check-out as August 2, 1934. However, that date did not appear on the erased and re-labeled check-out card to correspond to that August 2, 1934, first check-out date on the pasted-in check-out sheet opposite the card's pocket. Instead, the first date (with the user's name) which appeared on the check-out card was August 12, 1935, a year later than the first date on the check-out sheet (which showed no user's names). That certainly suggests that the check-out card did not originally match the check-out sheet, and that the copy may not have been on the shelves of the Columbia Teachers College Library for some time after August 2, 1934. However, both the check-out card in the pocket at the back, which presumably at one time was retained in the library when the book was checked out, and the check-out sheet showed that they had been erased and mislabeled, reading incorrectly Ayres' Spelling Scale instead of A Measuring Scale for Ability in Spelling. Neither showed the author's name, Leonard P. Ayres. The call number had also been erased and written in as 370.8, R. 91, No. 139.

It seems very possible that a discarded check-out sheet and card from two other books were re-used for this book. That certainly suggests the misfiling and mislabeling may have been done by some librarian at the college about 1934, who might well have been aware if properly identified copies of the Ayres scale had been disappearing from the stacks. "No. 139" was the Russell Sage Foundation number for that publication, so possibly the copy had been made part in 1934 of Columbia Teachers College Library's set of Russell Sage Foundation publications, numbering well over 100 titles. However, why did the check-out card and the card pocket not show the correct title, and why did they omit the author's name? My local librarian who requested the inter-library loan for me told me that the Teachers College Library had trouble finding the copy, which is hardly surprising. Therefore, that copy could not be found in the stacks after 1934 except almost by accident.

Was the altered state of the check-out pocket at the back of that copy and its altered title an attempt by someone at Columbia Teachers College in 1934 to frustrate the attempts of others there who had removed earlier copies of the Ayres scale from Columbia Teachers College Library? In 1995, even Buckingham's once-famous extension of the Ayres scale, obviously widely promoted nation-wide as a replacement for Ayres 1915 scale, was not to be found in the Columbia Teachers College Library, as the librarian there assured me by phone after checking their card files!

However, after some considerable effort, I had finally found a copy of the Ayres scale. At a Reading Reform Foundation meeting, I mentioned it to Mr. Mott of Mott Media and he told me he was interested in republishing it. I sent him photocopies of my photocopies, and Mr. Mott reset it in new print and republished it in 1986. He did not use the introductory material I had sent him and instead had someone shorten and rewrite it without my reviewing their product. Some of their rewritten content is wrong, but unfortunately it is signed with my name.

Since 1986, other printers besides Mott have reproduced copies of the original Ayres scale, which are now available in print and on the Internet. However, to my knowledge, none of those reproductions were available before 1986. So far as I have been able to find out, public mention or knowledge of the Ayres scale was effectively gone, from the early 1930's to 1986.

As has been discussed, public knowledge of both the excellent 1915 spelling scores and of the "high-frequency-word effect" posed a deadly public-relations threat to the success of the deaf-mute-method readers published about 1930. The evidence indicates that a very successful effort was made to remove that deadly threat, the public knowledge of the Ayres scale (and even the Buckingham version), just about the time that those deaf-mute methods arrived in the schools, which was shortly after 1930.

At the Library of Congress, all that survived of the Ayres spelling scale in July, 1981, when I was permitted personally to check the shelves there, was the cover of the Ayres spelling scale, on which the inside binding showed torn stitches where the contents had once been ripped out. The Ayres handwriting scale had been inserted into the empty cover, presumably to hide the loss of the sole Library of Congress copy of the Ayres spelling scale from the librarians when they made periodic shelf checks. Yet there were many copies on a nearby shelf of the Ayres handwriting scale, which suggested there had once been multiple copies in the Library of Congress of the Ayres spelling scale, as well.

I once held in my hands that cover of the sole Library of Congress copy of Ayres' A Measuring Scale for Ability in Spelling. It had once held the book, Part I, and probably the paper scale, Part II. With my own eyes, I saw the broken stitches on its inside binding where the original contents had been ripped out.

If it were simply theft, would a thief have gone to the trouble to insert Ayres' handwriting material into that spelling scale cover? No check is made at the Library of Congress when books are returned. An empty spelling-scale-text cover after the text was ripped out and replaced with something else could therefore have been placed on the return shelf in the middle of a pile of other books, or simply left in a pile of books on one of the hosts of readers' desks. The thief could then safely disappear. After all, the Library of Congress certainly could not attempt to replace the missing Ayres spelling-scale text if its clerks did not even know that it had been stolen.

Charles F. Heartman's third edition of his <u>Biographical Check List of the New England Primer</u> was published in 1934, his first and second having been published in 1916 and 1922. Samuel Blumenfeld wrote that Heartman reportedly remarked on the "most curious fact" that some of the primers listed in 1916 and 1922 could no longer be located by 1934, "probably due to the crime wave which spread, a few years ago, over all the libraries in the country." At the wishes of Krupskaya, Lenin's widow, periodic government-arranged "sweeps" of the Soviet Union libraries had been carried out there during the 1920's. (See Robert H. McNeal's biography, <u>Bride of the Revolution,</u> 1972.) However, it is manifestly true that any such library "sweep" carried out by unknown people in this country would be, indeed, a pure "crime wave". Did the original copy of that Ayres scale disappear during that recorded, early 1930's, criminal "sweep" of American libraries, or was it later?

It was no ordinary thief, probably some long time before July, 1981, who ripped the contents out of that sole surviving copy of the Ayres scale, and who then inserted the Ayres handwriting text, in order to hide the theft from the clerks returning books to their shelves. Instead of ordinary thievery, it appears to have been just one more instance, as with today's Mainstream Media, and with Krupskaya and her agents back in the 1920's, of a deliberately programmed attempt to control what enters the public mind.

Printed in the United States
by Baker & Taylor Publisher Services